Shaping My Feminist Life

MIDWEST 🌾 REFLECTIONS

Memoirs and personal histories of the people of the Upper Midwest

Shaping My Feminist Life

A Memoir

Kathleen C. Ridder

Foreword by Jill Ker Conway

Minnesota Historical Society Press • St. Paul

Midwest Reflections
Memoirs and personal histories of the people of the Upper Midwest

Manufactured in the United States of America

10 9 8 7 6 5 4 3 2 1

International Standard Book Number 0-87351-364-9 (cloth)
0-87351-365-7 (paper)

The paper used in this publication meets the minimum requirements of
the American National Standard for Information Sciences Permanence
for Printed Library materials, ANSI Z39.48-1984.

Library of Congress Cataloging-in-Publication Data

Ridder, Kathleen C., 1922–
Shaping my feminist life : a memoir / Kathleen C. Ridder ;
foreword by Jill Ker Conway.
p.   cm. (Midwest reflections)
ISBN 0-87351-364-9 (cloth : alk. paper). — ISBN 0-87351-365-7
(pbk. : alk. paper)
1. Ridder, Kathleen C., 1922–   . 2. Feminists — United States —
Biography. I. Title. II. Series.
HQ1413.R5A3   1998
305.42'092 — dc21
[b]   98-24413
CIP

All photographs are from the collection of the author.

For Rob

Contents

FOREWORD

⸎

Jill Ker Conway

Kathleen Ridder's memoir is a story of a woman who would not be radicalized. This theme is almost unprecedented among women's autobiographies, which since the 1950s have been focused on mother/daughter relationships, the quest for liberation from demeaning views of women, and the struggle for professional recognition. With the exception of the major polemical works of feminist leaders like Betty Friedan and Gloria Steinem, women have told their stories as narratives of personal relationships. Ridder's memoir is not easily classified in this context. She reports a satisfactory relationship with a competent mother, and her feminism seems to emerge more from her frustrated political interests than from a political analysis of her personal relationships. Nonetheless, her memoir tells us repeatedly about problems she experienced in her fifties and sixties because of the rage that would well up in her on feminist questions. Her work raises important psychological issues for the reader: Just what does radicalize women feminists, and why was Ridder's journey so different?

Kathleen Ridder tells her story in a characteristically strong voice. From the first page we hear a woman speak who has no hesitation in addressing her readers and who does not engage in the self-denigration so often instilled in women who have not had full-time professional careers. Her story has a firm ring to it, with none of the hesitations of the "I was just a poor housewife" school or version of the genre. It tells us why she grew up with such healthy self-esteem in the conservative 1930s and 1940s, when women were supposed to marry young, have lots of children, and submerge themselves in a husband's career.

Each new generation forgets the triumphs of its predecessors, but it is worthwhile pointing out that Ridder's generation, which came of age during the years of economic depression and world war, was the one for which all previous demographic trends were reversed. Up until the 1940s the higher a woman's level of education, the fewer children she had and the more time she spent in pursuits other than domestic work and parenting. But women who came of age in the 1940s were subjected to America's deep anxiety about providing enough work for men, an anxiety produced by the trauma of the Great Depression, when, at times, two-thirds of the male workforce was without employment other than make-work. This unemployment or underemployment was reversed only by the onset of global war in 1939, a fact that dominated planning for postwar demobilization. That was why women like Friedan and Kathleen Ridder experienced a culture that was sending them every possible message that a woman's place was in the home and that paid work for women was deviant, suspect, or selfish.

But Ridder had other messages that Friedan's life circumstances did not provide. First there was her mother, who, with Ridder's aunts, engaged in highly entrepreneurial work as fashionable couturiers, earned a handsome living, managed a family in style, and expected high achievement at two institutions devoted to raising aspiring women — the Brearley School and Smith College. Then there was marriage to Robert Ridder, surely one of the most engaging and sympathetic husbands in recent women's memoirs. The young Ridder ménage never consumed Kathleen Ridder's energies in endless housekeeping and child rearing, because there was money for household help and child care and because Rob

Ridder's job in the communications media of his well-to-do family opened the path for his wife's community involvement. It was part of the 1970s feminist rebellion to denigrate the use of household help and therefore require the surgeon or investment banker to clean her own toilet and change her own baby's diaper. Nothing could have been more destructive to the professional woman's career, because it is impossible to assume a male role without a home helper. Kathleen Ridder's upper-class world allowed for a wide range of paid support in her home and thus enabled the creativity that she brought to her restless and challenging volunteer career.

When one reads this memoir, it is hard to believe that Ridder (Smith, class of 1945) is a near contemporary of Betty Friedan's (Smith, 1943), for they seem to have inhabited totally different worlds. Ridder's prosperous working mother gave her daughter a different psychological climate to grow up in so that the early union that trapped Friedan in an unhappy marriage, and the suburban "problem that has no name," did not stunt Ridder's development. She had the sense of being one of the managers of the world, and she acted like it.

Nonetheless, Ridder experienced the problems Friedan defined, only in a different key. She was born to run things, but as a volunteer she kept being sidelined in the many organizations she worked in, just at the point where a paid professional would have been accorded major executive responsibility.

From the first years of her married life that began in Duluth, Ridder tells us how totally uncharacteristic of her generation she was. Describing the birth of her daughter, she writes of her refusal to sentimentalize motherhood: "I was surprised that happiness did not instantly envelop me when I held my infant to my breast for the first time. Instead, while I struggled

to get Kathleen to grasp my nipple, *no* maternal instinct overwhelmed me." She felt absolutely no guilt in handing the
baby over to a nanny. Both Ridder and her husband had been
brought up by nurses and governesses, and they took such
arrangements as natural and desirable. That left Ridder free
to finish her B.A. degree at Duluth State Teachers College,
combining her studies with a full complement of volunteer
activities expected of her. The classes brought her into contact
with a student body vastly different from those at Brearley
and Smith. These midwesterners were Democrats or Farmer
Laborites, and they inspired Ridder's political education. Getting to know them gave her the empathy that took her early
into the civil rights movement and fueled her energy for
urban politics. But she was a realist, never an ideologue:
"Emotionally, I sympathized with the problems of the lower
socioeconomic class. Intellectually, I knew I had married into
management. My bread and butter was there, and I had a
role to play as the wife of a Ridder." The role and the empathy with the oppressed were the two poles of a complex
personality, and Ridder's memoir is the more compelling
because of her open acknowledgment of the contradictions.

As soon as the young couple moved to St. Paul, the role
brought Ridder into civic life. The St. Paul Women's Institute,
on the board of which Ridder served, was the creation of the
Ridder family's St. Paul newspapers and their need to boost
advertising revenues from flagging downtown businesses.
Merchants and volunteer women combined to bring new
activity to downtown commerce, pulled there by the excellent
cultural programs run by the institute. This early link carried
Ridder into other civic activities and gave her a network in
the city unusual for a young mother still in her twenties.

She was not slow to use it. She held the old northeastern
elite's view of "politics as a civic responsibility," she tells us.

But for Ridder it was more than that. She saw political involvement as a way to "fulfill my quest to have a special life of my own, outside my role as wife and mother." Ridder writes this passage about her life in 1947, the time Betty Friedan was later to write about as the formative era of the "feminine mystique." Why was not Ridder a believer?

There are a number of points at which her life had given her many of the platforms on which to build a strong feminine identity and an easy association with power. Several times her narrative refers to the model of Ridder's mother and aunts and their thriving business. The business gave Ridder's mother access to networks of power through the shop's clientele. So from childhood Ridder had seen women use connections to achieve what they wanted. Her New York family was politically active; both males and females took working for the Republican Party as a matter of course. She married a man who was at ease with strong women, and whose family networks in the Midwest were just the kind Ridder had become used to in New York. Blessed with good health, and free from the psychological conflict Friedan was later to describe as what crippled women and left them no role but that of wife and mother, Ridder had prodigious energy for her quest.

There were important moments of self-doubt along the way, however. One of the biggest was the threat to their way of life presented by Rob Ridder's drinking. Ridder decided to enroll at the University of Minnesota to qualify as a secondary school teacher. She did well in her classes and valued the security that formal professional training gave her. She was satisfied that she could manage alone, albeit on a very different economic scale, if the marriage foundered on an alcohol problem. Just before graduation several very promising job opportunities were presented to her. She showed uncharacteristic hesitation on the brink of this decision. What would the Ridder circle think of a full-time working woman? Could she really do it? In the end the alcohol problem was mastered, Ridder never took a full-time job, and the crisis passed. She settled the issue for herself and for her supportive teachers at the university by getting pregnant, for in that era a pregnant woman teaching was out of the question. The reader cannot help wondering what school, school district, or educational system might have been transformed by Ridder's energies, or what master teacher might have become a model for her peers, had Ridder decided to take the risk.

So there were ways in which Ridder was a captive of the feminine mystique. Full-time work for a married woman was something she thought too revolutionary to try. This makes the story of her volunteer life one of causes and institutions embraced with drive and skill, accompanied by the recurring disappointment of discovering that, as a volunteer, she could not really run things. She could raise money, help to build buildings, shape new reform groups, and promote innovative educational ideas, yet there were limits to what she could make happen. Within those limits, however, her story is one of untiring effort on behalf of causes she always embraced ahead of her time.

In Minnesota politics Ridder became a delegate to the Republican State Convention, the Republican county chair-woman, and an alternate delegate to the 1956 Republican National Convention. But after a decade in which she had mastered the workings of the local, state, and national party system, she became bored by never-ending meetings and frustrated that she could not arouse her political associates to · the social and racial issues she thought important — the issues of civil rights and poverty that were to explode in the 1960s and 1970s.

In 1958, the Ridders both joined the St. Paul Urban
League and were well-established civil rights workers by the
time of the upheavals of the 1960s. She was working for
school integration well before legal challenges mandated
desegregation. Ridder learned to cope with being called a
"nigger lover" by clinging to the model of Eleanor Roosevelt,
the leader she'd secretly admired all through her childhood
when it was customary in her family's circle to mock Eleanor
and Franklin. That model told her it was good to fight for
social justice and equality despite social censure. Of course
people like the Ridders and other white liberals on the Urban
League board were soon bypassed by the Black Power movement, but the experience had heightened Ridder's sense of
social justice and made her willing to step out of line to support unpopular causes.

When Ridder's civil rights work brought her appointment to the state Board of Human Rights in 1969, she first
encountered complaints of discrimination in employment filed
by women. The work surely raised Ridder's consciousness,
but it was here that she also first experienced the problem
that was to plague her in her mature career: the staff of reform
organizations wanted the lobbying clout of someone with
Ridder's connections, but they didn't want her to define policy
or tackle issues publicly without one of them to watch over
her. Her identity as a white Republican woman from the suburbs, married to a wealthy and influential media executive,
kept getting in the way of her more liberal social perceptions.

Ridder did not bother to read Betty Friedan's *The Feminine Mystique* when it was published to broad acclaim. She
had not personally faced overt discrimination as a woman,
and she thought she was doing well as a volunteer and political activist. She seemed to be able to improvise an interesting
and highly educative life, moving on to a new cause when she

felt herself being sidelined in her efforts. Ridder worked for
the ERA and joined the Minnesota Women's Political Caucus, but she was not conscious of any way in which the issues
had an impact on her personally. For several years her attention focused on the Parks and Recreation Commission of her
suburban county, and then on its Planning Commission, of
which she became chair, relishing the personal power that
went with the position. Nonetheless, the messages of the
women's movement were getting to her, because in the early
1970s she decided that her next job had to be paid and that
she would seek nomination as a Republican candidate for the
Minnesota legislature, a pro-choice candidate in a predomi-
nantly "right to life" political environment. The cause was a
lost one from the start, but campaigning alerted Ridder to the
extent to which the political system was stacked against
women candidates, and the extent to which "women's issues"
received only token consideration. Moving out of the help-
ing volunteer role and into the role of direct contender for
power, in politics as well as other institutional hierarchies,
was almost radicalizing for Ridder, and the tension in the
remainder of her story is in the variety of ways she dealt with
that. Her interests were relentlessly carrying her beyond the
position of the elite volunteer who thought "other women"
had problems they were being too noisy about, to seeing that
she herself had many of the same problems. Like many women
in her generation, she suddenly remembered an instance of
sexual harassment that she had brushed aside. With that
memory came a degree of anger that surprised her. She was
one of many in her generation who suddenly became aware
in their fifties that they understood what the younger feminists of the 1960s and 1970s had been talking about.

What is unusual about Ridder's journey is the stubborn
determination with which she has worked to make existing

power structures meet feminist demands. For many American feminists, such efforts have led to bitter disillusionment. For Ridder, nowhere is that disillusionment more powerful than with the Roman Catholic Church, of which she remains a practicing member. She has dealt with it in her usual pragmatic fashion. She finds the liturgy sustaining and at times just blocks out the sermons. She makes clear that she is able to live happily with such contradictions, and the story of her unceasing activism shows that the effort to do so does not sap her energy. On the other hand, she is able to end her narrative on a far more positive note with her work in the area of women's sports at the university level. Thus, in her concluding statement, she describes not the sadness of the unfilled talent, the silenced voice, the cause lost because of discrimination, but a continued optimism that sustains belief in a political system that shortchanges women, because she has learned how to make trouble for those who try to pass her over. She also is fulfilled by watching the achievements of new generations in her family — a family she has never experienced as a constraint.

PREFACE

Like millions of women in the United States, I am proud to
call myself a feminist. In my view, to be a feminist is not
only to believe that women have social, political, educational,
religious, and economic rights equal to those of men, but
also to act on this belief to promote and defend these rights.

After seven decades on this earth, I often look back to see
how my choices have shaped my life as a feminist. It is clear
to me that many women's lives have been similar to my own.
We were born into families of comfortable means, and we
married men of considerable wealth, thus being indelibly
stamped as part of the social and economic stratum known as
"the privileged class." Most of us willingly fulfilled the traditional obligations placed on us to be active in civic, cultural,
and social arenas — as volunteers, of course.

For most of us, the transition from upper-class home-
makers and women behind the men into strong advocates
for women's equality was not precipitous. But as awareness
and opportunities grew, we began to realize new applications
for the skills we had acquired during our many years of
involvement in churches and schools, political parties, civic
endeavors, social agencies, and cultural organizations. When
we joined the women's movement, we brought along our
organizational abilities plus a long history of fund-raising
success — and we brought along our money.

For my part, I have chosen to support the goals of the women's movement by working within the established groups and organizations that have felt like home to me for many decades — places where I think I can make a difference.

From my vantage point, it is the volunteers in the women's movement who are the unsung heroes. We are the ones who set up the meetings from which emerged the leaders and strategies that pointed the way to the future. It is impossible to calculate how many women have given freely of their time. We are often referred to as "the mythical marching millions."

Let me introduce myself: I am a wife of fifty-five years, a mother of four, a grandmother of four, a practicing Roman Catholic, a Republican, and a confirmed feminist. I offer here an account of my activities — my successes and failures — in the feminist movement.

Shaping My Feminist Life

CHAPTER 1

I WAS BORN ON MANHATTAN ISLAND

In June 1943, I left my home in New York City and embarked on a six-day honeymoon and a new life. Twenty years old and newly married to Robert Blair Ridder, I saw myself as a twentieth-century pioneer woman leaving the hub of the world for unknown territory — Duluth, Minnesota. I came from a community of strong women. My mother and her two sisters ran a successful dress shop, Kathleen, Inc., not the typical role for women in their social and economic position. But I did not have the foresight then to know how these women were to influence my development as a feminist, nor did I foresee how my vision would be broadened beyond the narrow scope of an upper-class environment. My aspirations at that moment were to be a successful wife and mother, with the focus of my life contingent on that of my husband.

On our brief honeymoon trip, I saw more of my country than I had seen in all my life: a cab ride through Washington, D.C.; three days in Hot Springs, Virginia, a part of the South that, to my surprise, looked nothing like *Gone with the Wind*; a train ride through poverty-filled Appalachian mining country and rich midwestern farm fields; and a stop in Chicago for Rob's business and dinner at the famous Pump Room.

Rob and I had met through family connections at a dance in New York City. Like me, he was reared in the East. He had attended grammar school in the city and then went on to Portsmouth Priory, a Catholic boys' boarding school, and Harvard. Because of a lung condition he was deferred from active military service but had a temporary commission in the U.S. Coast Guard in Duluth. Since 1942 he had worked at the *Duluth Herald* and the *Duluth News-Tribune,* two of the family-owned newspapers published by his father, Victor Ridder.

Duluth, a city of just over one hundred thousand, clung to a steep incline rising from the western tip of Lake Superior. Its site afforded beautiful views of the impressive lake. Through the harbor steamed the long, flat ships that took iron ore from Minnesota's Iron Range to the steel mills of the East. From my new home I could watch the ships as they began their long voyage back through the Great Lakes. Although our house was small compared with my family's four-story brownstone in New York, I felt lucky to start out married life in it rather than in a one-room apartment, as many of my Smith College friends did. Most of them were engaged to men in the armed forces, and after marrying they would live out of suitcases, following their husbands from one military base to another.

In my two years at Smith there were no women's studies courses that could have put into perspective my mother's career as a businesswoman in light of the cultural norm, accepted by women, of subordinating their lives to their families. It wasn't until the women's movement and the establishment of women's studies programs at colleges and universities that I realized how much I had missed in my liberal arts curriculum. A few of us talked about careers, but there was a war going on and marriage was uppermost in our minds. On the other hand, because Smith was a women's college, we ran the student activities, which gave us ample opportunities to develop our organizational and leadership skills. When I organized the freshman Rally Day skating show, for example, I worked hard to fuse together the strong opinions of others who really thought *they* should be the director.

When I arrived in Duluth, my paramount interest was to get settled in my new home. Walking into our bedroom-to-be, I saw an oversized twin bed! I immediately suggested we stay at Rob's parents' summer home several blocks away until we could get some new furniture. To live at the home of Victor and Ruth Ridder — Mr. Ridder and Mumsie to me — was sheer bliss. Dorothy, the Norwegian housekeeper, took up her accustomed summer role at the Ridder home the day after our arrival. Dorothy did the cooking, cleaning, washing, and ironing. Elizabeth Hughes, the woman who took care of me as a child, would have described this as living like the Queen of Sheba. My only task each day was to discuss the menu and buy the food. This done, I walked or drove around Duluth. Getting to know the city in this way, I found that its architecture and tree-lined streets were similar to the suburban cities surrounding New York. The revelation gave me a feeling of security and comfort, as if I were not so far away from home after all.

When my friends in New York heard that I was to live in Minnesota, they responded with, "Oh, you are going to be among all those Scandihoovians!" It didn't take long to recall their comments after Dorothy served our first breakfast, where I declined coffee, which I don't like.

"You don't drink coffee?" she said, as if I had committed a cardinal sin. "That is all we drink here in Duluth. You'll have to learn to make coffee the way we do. We put eggshells in it while it brews."

I soon learned the role that coffee played in the social functions of Duluth's Scandinavians. Our first dinner invitation came from Ray and Elizabeth Van Horn. He was the general manager of the *Herald* and the *News-Tribune;* she was a very formal Norwegian woman. The meal was a sumptuous, and characteristically monochromatic, pork dinner with thick gravy, cauliflower, and scalloped potatoes, topped off with huge helpings of apple pie. When I politely refused coffee during dinner, Mrs. Van Horn was very surprised and said that it was a Scandinavian custom to have the coffee pot on the stove, ready to pour, when someone came to visit. The intimation was that if I were to fit in with the established social customs of Duluth, I'd better learn to like the drink. Custom or not, I never did.

Our social life increased after Mumsie and Mr. Ridder arrived for their summer vacation. Mr. Ridder was listed on the masthead as publisher of the *Herald* and the *News-Tribune,* but Ray Van Horn saw to the daily running of the papers. To build goodwill for the papers, the Ridders entertained a great deal. Because of wartime food rationing, they usually held cocktail parties, functions Rob and I regularly attended.

As the daughter-in-law of the publisher, I knew that I was expected to be gracious and acceptable to the movers and shakers of Duluth, to promote the city, and to participate in its social and civic life. At these gatherings, I learned that Duluth's residents had names other than Olson, Johnson, Lindstrom, Carlson, and Erickson. The Congdons, Blairs, Salyards, Alworths, Mitchells, Griggses, Heimbachs, and Welleses came to the house. Few of the younger members of these families were living in Duluth. Many of the young women were away at college or married to servicemen and living near military bases, and Rob and I were always the youngest people there. The older people were most gracious to me and asked the usual questions about my home and education. Rather than constantly say that I had grown up in New York City, I varied my answer by saying that I was born on Manhattan Island. If people looked quizzical, I would add, "A borough of New York."

I quickly realized that the social composition of Duluth was similar to that of New York. The wives of the couples resembled the mothers of my friends from St. Lawrence Academy (a small, Catholic coeducational school run by the Sisters of Charity) and from the Brearley School (an elite academy for girls). These women easily fitted into Mother's social circle and could have been customers at her store. There was, however, an important difference between Mother's life and theirs: she was a working woman.

Mother — Muriel MacGuire Culman — managed my aunt Kathleen's dress shop, housed in a renovated brownstone on East Sixtieth Street. She was born of Irish parents in the brownstone next door, where Aunt Kathleen and her husband continued to live. My father, Otto Culman, whose parents were of German stock, was a stockbroker who each day took the subway from our home on East Ninety-fifth Street to Wall Street. During the 1920s, he made a great deal of money in bank stocks but was devastated by the crash of 1929. Mother's salary was vital to ensure our way of life until the 1940s, when Daddy was again making money, although certainly not the huge sums of the prosperous twenties.

I was concerned about how to portray Mother to the women of Duluth, whose lives centered on family and exemplified the adage that the home was where women found true happiness. I feared that any of my shortcomings, perceived or otherwise, could be attributed to having had a working mother. But I was proud that Mother was a successful manager of a retail business with a staff of more than one hundred people, and prouder still that she was a married woman who was in love with her husband and had three normal, happy children.

My mother-in-law quickly solved my dilemma. Since Mrs. Ridder helped run her family-owned newspaper in New

Muriel MacGuire on her wedding day, 1921

My father and I, age four months, in 1923

Brunswick, New Jersey, she did not hesitate to point out that my mother was in business. At a cocktail party, she would say, "Oh, Muriel, Kathleen's mother, runs a very well known dress shop in New York—Kathleen, Inc." Women would enthusiastically ask me if this was the Kathleen's that advertised in the *New Yorker*, and I responded in relief with a quick yes. Because Mother managed an establishment that was successful enough to advertise in a national magazine, they recognized that she had achieved a certain status. My anxiety was assuaged.

With time, and the favorable response of my new community, I felt comfortable acknowledging that Mother worked. It added to my cachet as the new bride on the block. I emphasized that my childhood in New York was a normal and happy one, similar to a child's in Duluth. At times, people didn't believe me; they had a different impression of life in the big city. In fact, their idea of my youth was more perceptive than I realized. In my eagerness to establish my identity, I did not recognize the differences between life in New York and Duluth, although I would soon discover them.

I was determined to be a model wife and attend to the running of a home. When Mr. Van Horn suggested that I write a fashion column for the newspapers, I declined because no other young woman whom I had met was working outside the home, and also, I wanted nothing further to do with the retail fashion world of my mother.

My assumption that I could cut off all ties with the past was naive. I did not realize how my mother used her contacts with customers at the shop to move me into opportunities that led to this new life: Miss Covington's exclusive dancing school, the Brearley School, Smith College. After I was accepted at Smith, the college I was most anxious to attend (it never occurred to me or my peers to attend a coed institution), Mrs. Dwight Morrow, Mother's customer and the mother of Anne Morrow Lindbergh, wrote a letter to Smith (her alma mater) in support of my application for scholarship aid. For Mother, the shop provided all the connections needed to help fulfill her wishes for me to have an excellent education, to "marry well" (a euphemism for marrying money), and to marry a man who was both my intellectual equal and a

Catholic. She knew that money alone did not bring happiness, yet she was practical enough to warn that the lack of it was a cause of friction in a marriage.

My family had known the Ridders through the years. Rob's sister Gretchen, who modeled for a short time at the shop, arranged for us to attend a dance together. We fell in love, and fortunately, Rob matched Mother's qualifications for a perfect marriage; he had gone to Harvard, made ten thousand dollars a year, and was a Catholic.

Despite my commitment to the traditional mores of married life, I immediately saw how differently people were treated within Duluth's upper-class setting. Before my first visit to the Kitchi Gammi Club, a men's club with rooms and dining facilities, Rob informed me that there was a separate entrance for women, as well as a women's dining room. To begin with, I thought it was a bit of a lark. But when I was told that the men's grill at Northland Country Club was reserved for the men, except on Saturday night, and that only the men could play golf on Saturday and Sunday mornings during the summer, my antennae shot up. I was aware that there were men's clubs and country clubs everywhere that restricted women's participation, and that there were also clubs for women only, but I did not get married, and leave my home, family, and friends, to be left alone every weekend while my husband played golf with the boys.

After Rob had played golf on several consecutive weekends, he came home to find tension between us. Although I didn't say anything, he understood I was not pleased and he suggested that I take up golf. Knowing that I was competitive, and to encourage me, he sweetened the proposition with a challenge: "When you beat me," he said, "I'll give you a fur coat." To a young woman anticipating her first Minnesota winter with only a cloth coat, a fur coat was a welcome

Kathleen Marie Culman and Robert Blair Ridder, married on June 11, 1943, in New York City

prospect. I added the stipulation that Rob play with me on weekends, on the public course. He agreed. Because I couldn't challenge the social customs of the clubs, I used the power that I had to set about making my life with my husband a partnership.

Certainly, the circumstances surrounding our marriage made this easier. We were young and passionately in love. We were alone, without family or childhood connections in Duluth; due to the war, there were few of our contemporaries in the city. We had no one to talk to but each other, and we became each other's best friend. We were not only good at sports but also enjoyed watching them. When Rob became involved in the administration of hockey, I eagerly joined him in his work. It was easy to entwine our lives, and both of us made every effort to do so.

We moved into our home on Superior Street in late summer after our new beds finally arrived. The day after we moved, Sigrid Mitchell called me. She was a New Englander, a formidable woman with first-class organizational skills. She had been chair of the Women's Institute, an educational and community organization made up of volunteers, whose yearly programs of writers, journalists, and dance and music celebrities were sponsored by the newspapers. As chair of the war bond drive for Duluth, she asked me to call a list of women's organizations to staff bond booths for a week. I was pleased to work for the war effort, and I learned how to make "cold" phone calls to persuade volunteers to work — a skill that would prove useful all my life. Young and patriotic, I was taken aback when one organization's president refused my request. I persisted: "If you can't do it next week, how about the following month, when your organization doesn't have so many activities?" My questions were intended to imply, delicately, that it was one's patriotic duty to work in

the booth. It became a game not to let any organization off
the hook.

One day in late October, my telephoning was interrupted
by a call from Rob. He asked if I would like to have Archduke Otto that afternoon for tea. The archduke was in Duluth
as the October speaker for the Women's Institute. I answered
with an enthusiastic yes. Here was my first opportunity to
meet a member of royalty.

At the Brearley School, the modern European history
course had thoroughly covered the influence of the Hapsburg
monarchy of Austria through many centuries of European
history. The Hapsburgs were deposed as a result of World
War I; Otto had been the heir apparent. I had wept copiously
at the end of the 1938 movie *Mayerling,* when the affair of
Crown Prince Rudolf of Austria (1858–1889) and Baroness
Marie Vetsera ended so tragically with the lovers' suicides. I
was excited about having a guest in my new home who was
so intimately connected with European history and with a
famous royal romance of the nineteenth century. I couldn't
wait to tell my family and friends in New York that I had
entertained an archduke in Duluth.

I spent the afternoon preparing for the visit and was ner-
vous, but ready, when Rob and our guest came through the
door. The archduke was tall, smartly dressed in a dark suit,
and had an angular face topped with black hair. He kissed
my hand when he greeted me. I thought, how gallant — and
how like royalty! We sat down in the living room, and
between sips from my Crown Derby teacups, the archduke
spoke positively about the Austrian combat unit the United
States War Department had decided to establish. He
expressed his disappointment, however, that he had not been
chosen to lead that unit by the Austrian expatriates, who
remembered, too well, the Hapsburgs' autocratic rule. My

initial enthusiasm about the archduke cooled when I realized that he was just one of many exiled royalty trying to regain their thrones. I sided silently with the expatriates. Like the founders of our democracy, the people of Austria did not want to live under a monarchy, and it was difficult to sympathize with our guest. My husband and I listened politely but held our tongues. It was a relief when the tea ended and I could go back to my calls and my own efforts on behalf of my country.

That fall I expanded my war work by volunteering in the laboratory of Miller Hospital. Smith College had offered a course to train students as laboratory technicians, which I took in the second semester of my sophomore year. I did well in the sciences, at one point thinking I might be a doctor. I was dexterous and found it rewarding to do lab work, like making tissue slides for examination under the microscope. In the lab at Miller we did urinalysis, tested blood, and prepared slides.

Fall activities increased even more when I was asked to become a provisional member of the Junior League of Duluth. To meet the requirements of membership, candidates took an orientation course that acquainted them with the social, cultural, and civic organizations of the city. I enjoyed that very much, but was completely on edge when the talk among the other women, most of whose husbands were overseas, turned to their pregnancies. Because of Duluth's size, everyone within its social groups knew everyone else's business. Coming from a big city where there was more anonymity (and therefore more privacy), I resented the assumption that this sharing of one's private life was not only acceptable but expected.

Consequently, when I discovered at the end of October that I was pregnant, I vowed to keep it a family secret as long as possible. Much to my mother's and in-laws' concern, I chose a family physician to deliver our child, rather than an obstetrician. To prevent my pregnancy being a topic of conversation, I decided that if someone saw me in Dr. Countryman's office, she would not immediately assume that I was pregnant. I continued my daily activities as I would normally, including my lab work at Miller Hospital. But one afternoon, descending the steep stairs to the bus stop in an early March blizzard, I slipped. I decided then and there, war work or no, to quit rather than hazard a miscarriage. I was afraid that the family would attribute a miscarriage to the fact that I wasn't under the care of an obstetrician, who, in their minds, would have provided more thorough professional advice.

Along with my war work, an opportunity arose to strengthen my partnership with my husband. Rob's war duties expanded when he was made public relations officer for the Duluth Coast Guard. In that capacity, he ran the Coast Guard hockey team, the Heralds, which marked the beginning of his long association with the hockey world. The Coast Guard didn't have enough servicemen to form a team, so Rob spent a good deal of time on the telephone recruiting players from the Iron Range and the copper country of northern Michigan. I assisted with the telephoning, tracking down players and arranging transportation, all the while becoming familiar with the logistics of running a team.

The games were played at the Duluth Curling Club. While Rob took care of details for the team between periods, I stood in a corner of the warming room watching the crowd divide into male and female groups. Rather than join the women, I gravitated to the loud talk of the men. The provocative male banter was very much like the conversations between my mother and her two sisters discussing Kathleen, Inc. The topic was different, but these men and the women in my family used the same analytic skills employed in any competitive situation. The sisters spoke about whether there was greater demand that season for suits than dresses, who was a good salesperson, how war regulations restricted manufacturing, and how they did in relation to their competitors. The men evaluated the play — one team's need for a new goalie, the other team's need for better defense. They cursed the referees, and, although they sat in the stands, they were active participants in the game. The men's conversation seemed much more like familiar territory to me than that of the women, who talked about children, rationing, and the weather. Tuned in to the men's talk, I enlarged my knowledge of hockey, a new sport for me, and gleaned information that I later passed on to Rob during our postgame conversations in bed.

I learned something else that winter that greatly affected me. In mid-January 1944, Rob and I drove to Virginia, Minnesota, with one of his business friends. We reached Virginia in time for dinner and afterward went to a boys' basketball game at the high school. The gym was packed. The screaming of the fans, whipped up by girls leading the cheers, was deafening.

I was startled to see girls as cheerleaders for the first time in my life. There were no cheerleaders at the basketball games I had played in high school, and at Ivy League football games, boys led the cheers. But here, in far-northern Minnesota, were girls kicking up their legs as if they were in a chorus line and shouting at the top of their lungs. I couldn't wait to find out if their only role in sports was to support the boys. Between periods, I asked the woman next to me when the girls played *their* basketball games. "Oh," she replied, "the girls have no athletic teams like the boys. They're just cheerleaders." I thanked her, surprised and a bit shocked that the girls did not receive equal treatment in athletics in the public schools.

I was fully occupied with activities, and the winter passed quickly, which was a blessing in light of my pregnancy. We spent our second summer in Duluth back at the Ridders' because our house on Superior Street had been sold and our new house would not be vacant until mid-August. That summer we continued to work in tandem in the athletic world. Rob made me the business manager of the *Herald* and the *News-Tribune*'s baseball team. The newspapers underwrote the team in the amount of $500. Mr. Francine, the accountant at the *Herald,* set up the team's books and gave me a short course in accounting. The revenue from the games totaled $1,587.63; expenses came to $1,847.84, producing a loss of $260.21. I proudly returned $239.79, the amount remaining from the papers' initial contribution. To cut costs, we paid boys to return fly balls that went over the stands. When there were no boys, I, very pregnant, chased the balls myself. We gave the players a small stipend at the end of the season, the largest being $25. My husband received $2.50 when he suited up for one game. I was paid nothing to keep the books and chase fly balls, but I thought little of it at the time.

The newness of marriage and the stimulation that came from living in a new environment continued to gladden my life in Duluth that second summer. Even the war news improved. We had landed successfully in Normandy in June; the war in the Pacific progressed favorably, and there was a general feeling that the war would not last much longer. With relatives and friends at the front, Rob and I were naturally encouraged. And, we looked forward to being parents. Mother had taught me that pregnancy was a natural happening and that I should lead as normal a life as possible. At age forty-three, she had worked the day of the night my brother Peter was born. Following her example, I continued avidly to learn golf.

On weekends, Rob and I played at the public course in Lester Park. We were often joined by Reidar Lund, the sportswriter at the paper. He and Rob showed great patience when I, nine months pregnant, took five times as many swings as they to get to the green.

Kathleen was born weighing nine pounds and three ounces at 2 A.M. on July 28. At 6 A.M., the nurse brought my hungry baby in for her first feeding. I was surprised that happiness did not instantly envelop me when I held my infant to my breast for the first time. Instead, while I struggled to get Kathleen to grasp my nipple, *no* maternal instinct overwhelmed me. I certainly did not mirror the pictures in women's magazines of smiling mothers, cuddling nursing babies in their arms. Silently, I became suspicious of those happy portrayals of motherhood that I heard at Junior League meetings.

Fortunately, Mother, who had come to be with us for the birth of her first grandchild, understood my emotional state. She persuaded Dr. Countryman to discharge me earlier than normal, saying she would be at home to take care of me and my baby. Back at the Ridders', I relaxed and began to enjoy motherhood, giving my daughter her bath and loving her as she nursed. Mother was helpful to me, assisting me with the tasks of caring for Kathleen, as well as telling stories about her own first experiences with motherhood. She made me laugh, and knowing about her trials made it easier to stop expecting magic and to enjoy getting to know my baby and learning the skills I needed to care for her. Although Rob and I had named our daughter Kathleen, from the beginning we called her Chou-Chou, a French term of endearment that Mother had used with me.

Mother spent three weeks with us. I had been apprehensive about her stay because of a disagreement we'd had

during our visit to New York the previous Christmas. I had
telephoned her just before dinner one night to say we were
not coming home as expected, but would eat with Hank Ridder, Rob's oldest cousin, who was on Christmas leave.
Mother was furious. The gauntlet had been thrown down: I
had chosen the Ridders over the Culmans.

Rob had seven Ridder male cousins who were, or would
be, in the newspaper business. Because of the war, none had
been at our wedding. My husband's future was with the
Ridder family, not with mine, and I wanted no more confrontations. I decided at that point that when Rob and I were
in New York, we would stay with the Ridders; when I was
alone, I would stay with my parents. Mother and I never
wrote about the incident in our weekly letters, nor did I tell
her of my decision. Now that she was visiting, I feared it
might come up in our conversations, and I was loath to discuss it again. Mother had a saying to which she adhered in
this instance: "It's water over the dam. Forget it." It was a
relief to know that even as I began to loosen ties with my
family, and make choices they disagreed with, it would not
affect my relationship with my mother.

Mother left in mid-August; we moved into our house on
East Seventh Street; Dorothy came back to us, after having
spent her customary summer with the Ridders; and I settled
in to being a wife and mother. By winter the routine of Junior
League volunteer work, staffing war bond booths, attending
Women's Institute programs and symphony concerts, and visiting other young mothers with my new daughter was
beginning to pall. The society I moved in was very homoge-
neous, and I missed the diversity of New York. Kathleen,
Inc.'s workforce was a microcosm of the city's population,
with all races, colors, and creeds represented. Rose, the head
of receiving and shipping, was Jewish. Tib, the packer, was

black, as was Ruth, the stock girl. The fitters were French, Czech, German, Italian, and Mexican. The women in the workroom were of all races. The sales force was made up of white, mostly upper-class women who suddenly had had to make a living. Every economic stratum was represented among the employees — from Mary the shopper (she ran errands for the workroom), who was one step above the present-day bag woman, to the debutantes who modeled during the high season to earn "pin" money.

Absent, too, from my life in Duluth was intellectual stimulation. I missed school. I had always liked learning, beginning with my days with the sisters at St. Lawrence Academy. I wasn't an excellent student, but I was a good one. I enjoyed the companionship of my classmates and the structure of the school day. After a rocky start at Brearley (St. Lawrence had not prepared me to keep up with the advanced curriculum), I soon became a good student. My marks enabled me to receive scholarship aid during the five years I attended. I was elected a student government representative from my class each year and was class president the second half of my senior year. I also was immersed in the athletic program, spending hours in the gym shooting baskets with my friends.

At Smith I enjoyed the academic work and the freedom of living away from home in a college house. Nevertheless, at the end of my sophomore year, just prior to marriage, I thought I never wanted to see another textbook. That feeling didn't last long. Mother had early impressed on me the importance of both religion and education: "If anything goes wrong with your life," she said, "you can always fall back on your religion and your education to keep you going." The unfinished business of my education nagged at me.

When I returned to Duluth after a Christmas visit home in 1943, I called the College of St. Scholastica to inquire about taking a course in the second semester, as a part-time student. I thought it only fair to tell that Catholic institution that I was pregnant. Not only were they not receptive to having a part-time student, they certainly weren't interested in risking their reputation by having a pregnant one. If people saw a pregnant woman among the students, how could they possibly know if she were married?

Unable to begin classes, I continued to satisfy intellectual pursuits with a self-taught Russian history course and by reading novels by Leo Tolstoy, Fyodor Dostoyevsky, and Ivan Turgenev. Rob had majored in Slavic studies at Harvard and was there to act as my tutor when I needed help.

By the fall of 1944 I was, again, itching for more. Our brief summer friendship with Sinclair Lewis, who was in Duluth to write *Cass Timberlane,* had heightened my awareness of the lack of mental stimulation. Lewis had taken a shine to us, principally, we thought, because Rob agreed to play chess with him, and Lewis used Rob as a chauffeur to drive him to social affairs. After returning from a social gathering, Lewis would ask us in for a nightcap. While he sipped coffee, Rob had a drink, and I nursed a soft drink, Lewis would satirize the other guests who had been at the function. He mimicked their dialogue perfectly, and displayed phenomenal perception with regard to the character of the people. At times, his insights seemed cutting, but his comments were a lesson in human psychology. Knowing an author was a new experience for me, and it was as enlightening as it was engaging. It helped broaden my ability to sense and understand people's motives. The friendship terminated when Lewis accused my in-laws of being rude to his newest girlfriend. In his diary he wrote tersely, "End of Ridders."

I took a University of Chicago correspondence course. My papers came back marked with Bs and As, but I craved human contact with students and professors, connections with people who were not necessarily of my social and economic group. Close by our home, on East Fifth Street and Twenty-fourth Avenue, was Duluth State Teachers College (DSTC). I enrolled that winter quarter in European history. The class met four mornings a week for an hour. Thrilled to be back in the classroom, I continued that course during the spring quarter and added an English literature survey.

In April 1945, I went to New York for three weeks with Chou to show her off to the MacGuire, Culman, and Ridder relatives. I wrote Rob that I was constantly having lunches and dinners with relatives, and couldn't wait to get back to Duluth to be alone with him and to study. Mother was particularly pleased that I wanted to get my degree, and she urged me to make every effort to graduate.

With her encouragement, and my own powerful wishes to get back to my studies, I decided that my goal for the next several years was to finish the course work for my junior and senior years, and to graduate from DSTC. On the train ride back from New York, I persuaded Mrs. Hall, whom I had hired for the trip, to stay with us on a full-time basis. I knew that her excellent help caring for our daughter would free me to focus on my educational goals. Neither my husband nor I felt guilty that I wasn't in complete charge of Chou; we had both been brought up by nurses and governesses.

I enrolled summer quarter in a childen's literature course taught by Mabel Culkin, the sister of the famous author Margaret Culkin Banning. Of course, she asked if I was a member of the publishing family, and when I answered yes, I realized that my cover was blown. Now, when Mabel told Margaret that I was in one of her classes, I would surely be asked at social functions about being in school. As no other woman of my social group was a student, it was obvious that I did not conform to the mainstream of Duluth's married women. If the question arose, I would explain that my parents hoped that after marriage I would make every effort to get my degree. Neither the times nor my social role would have allowed me to say that playing the part of a Ridder wife and daughter-in-law did not completely satisfy me.

For two quarters I had attended classes unnoticed. I was the right age, I dressed in the same skirts and sweaters as the other girls in class, and I looked and acted exactly like a budding schoolteacher who needed a job after graduation — an easy role to play because early on my parents had instilled in me that I was to make my own way after my education was finished. No other professor or student ever inquired about my background or made any comments as to why I was in school. In my final quarter, Dr. Charles Saltus of the English department did say that I was one of the few students who had come from another college whose marks had risen so perceptibly.

DSTC was the first public academic institution I attended. Candidates for admission were only required to have a high school degree; the tuition was ten dollars a quarter with an eight-dollar activities fee. The student body was egalitarian and populist rather than elitist. Being among these students expanded my contacts with the sons and daughters of union members, farmers, and small business owners, a very different sphere from the one I moved in as a member of a family that owned newspapers.

How did I deal with this dichotomy? I did not express opinions that might conflict with or support student ideas. Most of the students were Democrats or Farmer-Laborites. I was a Republican but was silent in class about my political allegiance. In political discussions with our friends, I often came across not as a conservative Taft Republican but as a moderate. Listening to the students gave me a greater understanding of the forces that sway politics in our country.

This is not to say that I had previously been isolated from the opinions of the working class. The International Ladies' Garment Workers' Union had tried numerous times to organize the women at Kathleen, Inc., but the union repeatedly lost the elections because Aunt Kathleen and Mother treated their employees well and paid them fair wages. I had read how women workers had been exploited by clothing manufacturers in the early 1900s and about the terrible Triangle Shirtwaist Company fire of 1911. Emotionally, I sympathized with the problems of the lower socioeconomic class. Intellectually, I knew I had married into management. My bread and butter was there, and I had a role to play as the wife of a Ridder.

Even though I often had to hold my tongue, I was not passive. I played this role at DSTC until March 1946, when the controversy over the future of the college came to a head. Dr. Herbert Sorenson, its president, led the drive to transform DSTC into a liberal arts college and a branch of the University of Minnesota. Many members of the faculty, the State Teachers College Board, and the cities where other teachers colleges were located, were greatly opposed to this change. My opinion was that the people in the opposition were simply protecting their turf: old, conservative professors (four of whom were publicly identified) might have to upgrade their courses; the State Teachers College Board would lose a member, thereby decreasing its power; and the cities with other state teachers colleges would envy the fact that Duluth would get the benefits of having a branch of the university.

What those opposed to the change also failed to realize, it seemed, was that the composition of the student body had changed, even since I had first enrolled. On June 22, 1944, Congress passed the GI Bill of Rights (the Servicemen's Readjustment Act), which gave returning veterans five hundred dollars a year for their education. Enrollment at DSTC had grown from three hundred to about eight hundred. By March 1946, many veterans were studying at the college, and they wanted bachelor's degrees — not teaching degrees.

I sided with the students who supported Sorenson and joined the organization of a student strike that took place on March 13. This was the first time I had joined a cause. The next day, at a school assembly, Dr. Sorenson read his letter of resignation. Even as he was reading, I cried. He was by far the best teacher I had had, and in my mind, he was the scapegoat of the opposition.

When DSTC officially became a branch of the university in the summer of 1947, I had learned a valuable lesson: you must always keep your sights on your ultimate goal. Dr. Sorenson had to resign, but the University of Minnesota–Duluth was established, a vindication of our efforts.

With the end of the war, the circumstances of our lives in Duluth changed. Jane and Bernie Ridder (an older cousin of Rob's), who had lived in the city for several years before Bernie entered the service, returned in the fall of 1945. Bernie became general manager of the newspapers, and Rob returned to his main interest in radio when he was named manager of WDSM, the radio station newly acquired by the family.

Rob's new business career did not take anything away from his interest in hockey. At the conclusion of the 1944–1945 hockey season, the Duluth Heralds team folded. Rob then became vice president of the Northern Amateur Hockey League in 1945, and two years later was made presi-

dent of the Minnesota Amateur Hockey Association and a
director of the American Hockey Association.

With Jane, another Ridder, in Duluth, I no longer felt as
obligated to participate in all the Women's Institute activities.
My volunteer work of getting women to staff the bond booths
came to an end. My hours of service as a provisional member
of the Junior League had been satisfied, and I was now a full-
fledged member. With my responsibilities as a Ridder wife
lessened, I was even more able to become a full-time student
and persuaded Mrs. Hall to stay on another year. Recollections
of my days during that year are a blur of attending classes in
the morning, taking care of Chou for two hours in the afternoon while Mrs. Hall had time off, studying in the evening,
and sometimes going to parties or entertaining at home.

At the end of this time, on June 4, 1947, I marched up to
the podium to receive my B.A. from DSTC, graduating at the
head of my class of ninety-nine. When I wrote to Mother to
tell her the graduation date, I urged her not to come because
Daddy had just been diagnosed with leukemia. (He died a
year later after having many blood transfusions that rejuve-
nated him for short periods of time, only to have the effects
wear off and leave him weaker than ever.) Mother had no
sooner received the letter than she was on the phone to say
that nothing could keep her from my graduation. She wanted
to celebrate with me, after all her years of encouragement,
my being the first female of the MacGuire clan to earn a college diploma.

Mother and Rob attended my graduation ceremony, and
the three of us marked the occasion with dinner at Northland
Country Club. During dinner, Mother handed me a gift-
wrapped box, saying with tears in her eyes, "You have no
idea how proud Daddy and I are of your achievement." Fifty
years later, I still wear the gold choker, a memento of my

parents' happiness at my academic success. And I was equally glad to have that diploma.

My graduation brought to a close our four years in Duluth. Rob and I had decided to move to St. Paul at the end of June, as he wanted very much to work at WTCN in Minneapolis. The radio station, located in a much larger market than Duluth, afforded a greater opportunity for Rob to increase his knowledge of the business. In addition, the Twin Cities area provided better possibilities to expand into television, the medium of the future. Rob also planned to extend the family interests in radio and television into markets where they already owned newspapers, such as Aberdeen, South Dakota, and Grand Forks, North Dakota. The convenience of air travel from the Twin Cities was far greater than in Duluth.

Mother's visit for my graduation also made our departure from Duluth easier. Parties were given both in her honor and as a farewell for Rob and me. Mother had developed friendships with several women she had met in Duluth. She had entertained them in New York, and they were delighted to return her hospitality on this visit. So often I heard her say at gatherings, "Oh, Kathleen is going to miss Duluth. Everyone has been so gracious and warm and made her feel so welcome when she arrived in your city as a bride. She and Robbie have had a wonderful time here!" I, too, was telling people how much my husband and I would miss Duluth, and having Mother repeat my thoughts in her charming and gracious manner gave them all the more emphasis.

It was during this visit that I recognized Mother's remarkable skill in dealing with people. I watched her being introduced at parties and immediately putting everyone at ease by saying with enthusiasm, "Kathleen has spoken of you in her letters." She could work a room like no one else, always finding a common thread in a conversation that identified her with that man or woman. What I did not recognize at the time was that Mother had always been my role model, providing, among other things, an example of how to lead a dual life. She had long played the role of wife and mother, and then detached herself to become a woman with a business career. Intuitively, I had stepped out of my social group to become a student at DSTC, and I did so with confidence. Like Mother, I welcomed new faces and places, and her example served me well, as it would continue to do in the next phase of my life.

Duluth had been very good to me. The size of the city enabled me to get around easily. From home, it took little time to reach our church, the supermarket, the country club, downtown, and the college. The close proximity of DSTC permitted me great flexibility in arranging my courses. As the daughter-in-law of the newspapers' publisher, I had been thrust into the city's social and civic life. Although these could have been difficult circumstances, I found that in four years, I had learned how to have a life of my own at the same time I melded it into the social framework of being a wife and mother in a prominent family. With my newfound knowledge, and the confidence I had gained juggling all my roles in Duluth, I looked forward, with great anticipation, to the challenge of a new life in St. Paul.

CHAPTER 2

❧

An Eastern Accent among the Cornfields

Buoyed by our happy years in Duluth, Rob and I arrived in St. Paul confident that we would create a life in our new environment as satisfying as the life we had led in that northern city. I looked forward to buying a home and forming a new circle of friends. As a member of a prominent family, I anticipated being an active part of St. Paul's civic and social life. It was also an upbeat time in our country's history. Following the Allied victory in World War II, factories produced the myriad washing machines, stoves, furniture, baby clothes, and cars needed to satisfy the demands pent up during wartime. Newly constructed homes appeared magically in new suburbs. In 1947, St. Paul boasted just over three hundred thousand inhabitants. Altogether, roughly one million people formed the large urban community of the Twin Cities. Rob's office was at WTCN in Minneapolis, and we were to live in St. Paul, where the family's major holding was the *St. Paul Pioneer Press* and the *St. Paul Dispatch* newspapers.

Immediately after our arrival, Agnes Kennedy Ridder, Uncle Ben Ridder's new wife, took me on a tour of St. Paul, beginning with the most impressive of its residential streets, Summit Avenue. The architecture — ranging from baronial to Tudor, colonial, and Victorian styles — resembled the homes of virtually any midwestern city of the same size. But a drive along the street's eastern reaches presented a visual history of the city: each of the large mansions either had been, or was still, occupied by one of the families that had shaped St. Paul.

Homes lining the avenue belonged to the Hill family of railroad fame; the Weyerhaeusers, lumber barons; and the Ordways, who had large holdings in Minnesota Mining and Manufacturing.

In a short time, Rob and I fell into the social pattern of an upper-class couple, mingling with the sons and daughters of those families who lived along Summit Avenue. We rented a house for the summer on nearby Osceola Avenue. At social gatherings I met local women my age as well as women who had come from the eastern United States as war brides. Many of them became my lifelong friends. In early July we joined the Somerset Country Club in suburban Mendota Township, where I played golf in the mornings. Three-year-old Chou-Chou went swimming every afternoon in the pool, and on late summer evenings Rob and I often golfed together, ending with dinner at the club. I felt very much at home living this life, so similar to the country club summers of my childhood. Actually, I was quite mesmerized by it, mainly because my golf game improved significantly. I won the Club Championship for Women and played for the club in the Women's City A League. In a round at the Town and Country Club in St. Paul, I beat Rob and finally won the fur coat he had promised me in 1943.

When not on the golf course, I house-hunted. Having experienced the "small townness" of Duluth, I did not want to start life in the Twin Cities living cheek by jowl with my neighbors. St. Paul had a much larger population, yet already I had observed that the social structure revolved around the graduates of Summit School and the St. Paul Academy. Rob and I wanted to be part of that group, but not immersed in it. Before the war, some families had moved southeast from the city to northern Dakota County, where they combined living in the country with proximity to St. Paul's business district. There in Mendota Township, we found our house.

It was a large, four-square, three-story structure built of Minnesota limestone, set on a hill surrounded by farmland in all four directions. The house was beautifully constructed and perfectly situated to satisfy my father's admonition to buy a house whose main rooms enjoyed daylong sun. On a glorious fall day, in the first week of October, we moved from our rented house into our new home. The weather matched my mood—exultant! Walking around the house I was struck again by how beautiful its location was. The warmth of the day enveloped me, and I was enthralled by the richness of the land. In my romantic musings as a twentieth-century pioneer bride moving to Minnesota, this was how I had envisioned the North Star State. Duluth's geography, a cool port city located on a rocky hillside that rose steeply from Lake Superior, had been such a disappointment—especially compared with this. My concepts and images of the prairies had come from the works of one of my favorite novelists, Willa Cather. I had read *My Ántonia* several times, and I admired Ántonia's

Our house in the 1930s

independent spirit and her resilience in overcoming adversity. Her strength came from the land. At that moment, I, a city-bred woman standing on our newly acquired acres, experienced its strength. I felt at home.

Having settled into our home, Rob and I devoted time to the civic life of St. Paul. Rob represented WTCN and became very active in the Red Cross and the Community Chest (the forerunner of the United Way). In October, Agnes Kennedy Ridder, who was executive director of the Women's Institute, asked me to become a board member and I accepted with alacrity. I had surmised from earlier family conversations that the St. Paul Women's Institute, in contrast to its Duluth counterpart, played a pivotal role in the success of the St. Paul newspapers. It seemed clear that the commercial market in Superior, Wisconsin, Duluth's next-door neighbor, did not offer a competitive threat to Duluth merchants to the same extent that the stores in Minneapolis challenged those in St. Paul.

The idea for the Women's Institute had originated nine years earlier, in 1938, with Bernard H. Ridder (Uncle Ben or B. H.). He had arrived in St. Paul to find that the newspapers were not making a satisfactory profit. Advertising dollars were the lifeblood of the industry, and St. Paul merchants were not investing theirs in ad space because women streamed across the Mississippi to shop in Minneapolis. No one had been able to reverse the pattern. B. H. called a meeting of prominent women in which Agnes Kennedy, whom he later married, said that women did not like to be told where to shop, but if there were good reasons to buy in St. Paul, they would. The newspapers surveyed five thousand women to determine why they did not shop in the city, and teams visited stores to gather information to present to a large group of store owners. This stirred the merchants into action, and, within a year,

$16 million was spent to refurbish the stores and improve the merchandise.

Meanwhile, the newspapers underwrote the institute's cultural program, the goal being to entice St. Paul women to shop downtown on designated "Institute Days." The cultural program was a series of seven afternoon and evening performances, presenting famous artists and well-known speakers. The cost of an institute membership entitling a woman to attend these events was $2.40, and membership was limited to women who lived in St. Paul. To enable out-of-town guests to participate, St. Paul women were encouraged to buy gift memberships, which included invitations to these events (though women in Minneapolis were not included).

The high quality of the institute programs had started with opening night, September 20, 1939, when Eleanor Roosevelt spoke about the responsibility of the individual to the community before an audience of twelve thousand in the St. Paul Auditorium. At the time I joined the board in 1947, the programs were of that same caliber, and the original format for Institute Day was still in place. Participating stores presented style shows, and women from various groups decorated the store windows around a theme (chosen by board members), such as a Sunday brunch, an afternoon tea, or a hunting dinner; the displays were judged. After eight years, the stores continued to be enthusiastic about the role the institute played in the economic life of the city, for it still brought nearly twelve thousand women to the downtown shopping area.

Even though I was a Ridder and my involvement was assumed, it was an honor to be a member of a board with a well-recognized tradition of working for the community. I called few of the members by their first name, which would have been forward of me because some of them were my mother's age. Eager to please, I worked as a "gofer" for the older women, whether it was on the style-show committee or the committees to decorate the auditorium stage or store windows. In time, the board members became nearer my age, and I worked with them on a more equal footing. I never chaired a committee, however. I agreed with Agnes that one Ridder in a leadership position was enough. Eventually, the routine of board meetings bored me, and the thrill of attending institute programs and meeting artists and celebrities flagged. As a member of the family, I could not resign, so I quietly withdrew from attending every monthly board meeting, citing conflicts with other board meetings and political work as my reason.

My interest in the institute was reactivated a number of years later when board member Gerry Seldon requested that I join the committee working to renovate Rice Park in downtown St. Paul. Agnes Ridder had spoken to the board in 1962 about her desire to commemorate the institute in the city. She suggested that the renovation of Rice Park would be fitting, as it would reflect a primary institute goal: the beautification of the city. This project appealed to me because it had a beginning, a middle, and a purposeful end. It was creative, in contrast to the routine activities of the institute, which were repeated year after year. The block-square park, opposite the old federal court building, was to be beautified with all deliberate speed. The project was a public-private effort and was my initial encounter with such an endeavor. I pored over landscape architects' plans generated by a statewide contest and tried to visualize the final product. One plan proposed that the entire square block be paved in red brick. I thought that was a spectacular idea, but was immediately told that it was beyond our budget. We had raised $150,000, with great effort, and the largest share was to go toward a fountain with a

statue in the middle. Alonzo Hauser, professor of art at
Macalester College, agreed to sculpt a female figure for a rea-
sonable sum. When the committee first viewed Professor
Hauser's clay model and discovered it was a nude, they exclaimed in horror that she had to be clothed. I could not
believe it. Most of these women had been to Europe and seen
many nude statues adorning public spaces and buildings. The
committee was so overwhelmingly in favor of shrouding the
figure in light garments, however, that I dared not voice a contrary opinion. I had misjudged: clearly, the members' acceptance of artistic nudity did not extend from Europe to public
display in St. Paul. But when Agnes, on further examination
of the model, objected to the thickness of the legs and the size
of the feet, I was unable to contain myself. In a voice that was
probably too loud, I pointed out that she was not a dainty
ballerina but a pioneer woman who worked in the fields. In
my mind's eye, I had a picture of Ántonia. I won that point.

On a sunny spring day in 1964, with the committee
standing in a circle around the fountain and Agnes acting as
master of ceremonies, the dedication of the renovated park
took place. Mayor George Vavoulis spoke to the crowd,
seated in bleachers, about "what the power of organized
women in our community can accomplish." Neither I nor
other board women thought then of women's power in the
sense that the phrase was later used in the women's movement, namely, to bring about change on behalf of women. I
did not yet acknowledge that I — or any other woman — had
power. We were all simply fulfilling our civic duty to improve
our city, as we had been taught. Our husbands were execu-
tives of city businesses. A vibrant city was essential for the
economic success of those businesses. This was what we
worked toward.

Women's Institute members at the dedication of Rice Park, 1964.
(Agnes Kennedy Ridder is in the middle; I am second from the left.)

The Women's Institute was a harbinger of the women's movement. Later in life it became clearer to me that institute activities enabled women to organize into a powerful force when they were given ownership and membership in an organization with an appealing mission. The experience taught me that to bring about change, one needed a critical mass of supporters and the financial backing to generate the numbers. The institute's membership was sustained because the newspapers bankrolled the programs until 1971, which was the last season of the organization. By that time, not only had television brought artistic celebrities into the living room, effectively reducing membership, but the fees needed to pay artists and speakers had become prohibitive.

In my early years in the Twin Cities area, the institute gave me the opportunity to connect with the problems facing an

urban environment. At the same time, working in politics, I
was thrust into the rural life of Dakota County, where we
lived. The end of World War II brought an explosion of interest in politics among those of us in the upper classes who were
living in the newly developing suburbs. We felt it was our
obligation to participate, for if we did not, the party hacks
would take over. Several of our friends became members of
city councils and school boards. I viewed politics as a civic
responsibility and a unique opportunity to be at the cutting
edge of a postwar movement and to fulfill my quest to have a
special life of my own, outside my role as wife and mother.

Both Rob and I had been interested in politics before the
war, Rob more actively than I; he had gone to the 1940
Republican National Convention as a Wendell Willkie supporter. That fall, back at Harvard, he worked for Willkie's
campaign. My family worked for Willkie in New York. During the 1940 Republican convention, I sat glued to my radio.
I heard the youthful Harold Stassen's rousing keynote address
and listened to the commentators as they described his political acumen in masterfully manipulating the delegates' votes
over to Willkie, who won on the sixth ballot. I was impressed
by Stassen, who had become governor of Minnesota at age
thirty-two. After the war, I had followed reports about Stassen's participation at the San Francisco Conference in 1945.
I admired his stance on the United Nations, for I wanted a
world order that ensured peace. Harold Stassen grew up in a
house on South Robert Street in West St. Paul, about two
miles from our new home. That added to his appeal, because
we were now geographically associated; he came from my
county, and he was a Republican.

My chance to become active in politics came in February
1948. Kay Harmon, who lived in nearby Sunfish Lake and

was married to Reuel Harmon, president of Webb Publishing Company, called to tell Rob and me when and where the Republican precinct caucus was to be held in Mendota Township. Kay, older than I by about ten years, was an attractive, intelligent New Englander, and in her imperious way, she implied that we would surely attend. She also urged us to become elected delegates to the county convention. Of course, we knew no one at the caucus, and during the nomination of delegates I was on pins and needles, anxiously wondering why no one nominated Rob or me. Could they not see we were young and eager? Or was it because I was quite pregnant, and they thought I would not or perhaps should not be interested in political activity? Just the opposite was true. I wanted some meaningful activity to pass the time until my due date at the end of May. When only two more people were needed to fill out the delegation, we were finally asked if we would like to go. Naturally, we agreed.

At the county convention in Hastings, I felt very uncomfortable, like a visible outsider from the sidewalks of Manhattan, with no experience of life on a farm. I was surprised, too, to see that the farmers were dressed in suits. I had expected the men to be in overalls and flannel shirts. The women dressed conservatively, in dark dresses or suits, and the delegates appeared to be prosperous farmers or merchants from the county's towns and cities.

Kay Harmon suggested that I run to be an alternate delegate from Dakota County to the Second Congressional District and state conventions. If I rounded up support among the delegates from Mendota, she would nominate me. I was complimented and felt fortunate that Kay, who knew the ins and outs of politics, had become my mentor. She taught me the basic lesson of politics: to be elected you had to have a

nominator and supporters to vote for you. Much to my
amazement, my fellow caucus members, attuned to the game
of politics, were not the least bit put out when I asked for
their support. Consequently, I won my first election and
eagerly awaited the district convention in Mankato.

Driving south with Kay and Hildur House, a delegate
from West St. Paul, to Mankato, I received another lesson in
politics: I was to participate in a "deal." Immediately, the
word *deal* made me feel sullied, as if I were to be used as a
pawn. But as Kay proceeded with her succinct explanation of
why I was to vote for "Doc" Radabaugh if I were seated as a
delegate, the give-and-take of the agreement began to emerge
as less tainted. I pacified my secret emotional reaction with the
thought that if Kay, a respected member of the community
and the Republican Party, accepted the bargain, it behooved
me to try to see the positive in it. Obviously, politics was a
competitive game, and players must strategize to win. Recon-
ciled to that given, I relaxed in the backseat of the car and let
my newfound zest for politics continue to wash over me.

The next stop on my new political journey was the state
convention in St. Paul. I applauded vigorously when Mrs.
Chris Carlson, the National Committeewoman, spoke with
pride about the fact that Minnesota was the only state sending a male and a female as delegate and alternate from each
congressional district to the national convention in Philadel-
phia that June. It seemed obvious that women should have
equal representation, although clearly that opinion was not
widespread. In my limited political career, I had not yet noticed
any gender discrimination, but I filed away Mrs. Carlson's
statement for future reference.

On June 21, 1948, I found myself in the press box (Rob
had press passes) at the side of the speaker's platform, over-
looking the delegates and alternates seated on the floor of the

national convention. The delegations were in rows designated by their state sign. Some wore straw hats on whose bands was printed the name of their favorite candidate. To leave absolutely no doubt as to whom they favored, gung ho delegates filled every available space on their jackets with campaign buttons. The edge of the balcony was festooned with American flags, hung like open fans. It was a festive, patriotic atmosphere, full of promise and energy.

After the first day and a half of the convention, my enthusiasm began to wane. The speeches droned on. The band music for each candidate's demonstration blared louder and louder. It became obvious that Thomas E. Dewey, not Harold Stassen, would be the nominee. Of the many speakers, only Clare Booth Luce, the playwright, editor of *Vogue,* and former member of the House of Representatives from Connecticut, impressed me. Married to Henry Luce, the publisher of *Time, Life,* and *Fortune,* she was charming, gracious, and beautiful. Her tailored, flower-print dress and natural straw toque contrasted with the conservative attire of the Taft and Dewey female supporters. As a politician, she appealed to me immediately. With her well-known wit and mastery of the English language, she captivated the audience and had us in the palm of her hand when she called President Harry S. Truman "a gone goose."

Invigorated by her speech and the general excitement of the convention, I boldly set a goal on my return home: to become the county chairwoman. I wanted to test my ability to lead in the political arena, and county chairs had political power. They ran the party structure, and, with the county committee, they devised plans for winning elections. Because elections take place every two years, with downtime between campaigns, my political development over the next four years happened in fairly concentrated periods. This schedule of episodic, but intense, commitment enabled me to lead a political life in harmony with my social and civic lives.

Social scientists would call our home life typical of upper-class suburbia in the 1950s. Our family grew with the addition of Robbie on May 26, 1948 (just in time for me to attend the Republican National Convention), and Peter on February 25, 1953. The children went to Catholic schools. We wanted them to be well grounded in their religion, even though the Catholic schools could not compete academically with other private institutions. In their large classes, the children made friends with peers who were not necessarily from the upper class. We believed that learning to mix with children from all backgrounds enriched their lives and was part of growing up in a democracy. Rob and I benefited immeasurably from our various activities that were not centered in one locale. Our social friends, by and large, were in St. Paul. Politically, our center of activity was the rural Second Congressional District. Civically, we worked in St. Paul, and Rob's business, now in both radio and television, was in Minneapolis.

Danila Boschello and Lillian Giles were the mainstays of our household. Danila lived with us, and Lillian came part-time to help with the cleaning and cooking. Mother found Danila in New York to take care of Chou and Robbie while we went to Europe in 1950, and the children had fallen in love with her. Fortunately, she accepted my offer to work in Minnesota. She had learned to be an exceptionally good cook in her family's restaurant in Italy. For many years, it was Danila who prepared the spaghetti and meatballs and salad that we served to more than 150 guests at our annual Christmas skating parties. Because of Danila and Lillian, I could depart for meetings and social affairs with the secure knowledge that all was under control at home.

Every other Tuesday during the school year I had lunch with the "Sewing Group," which gathered in members' homes, ostensibly to sew, knit, and mend. Actually, it was the lively conversation (at times just plain gossip) and common interests that brought the twelve of us together. I looked forward to being with friends who were intellectually and socially compatible. In those days, if I had called our get-togethers a women's support group, I would have been hooted out of the room — we saw ourselves as independent women who needed no support. The women were active in the arts, music, social issues, and politics in various leadership positions. For example, Constance Otis was state chairwoman of the Republican Party, and Barbara Bemis was chairwoman of the Upper Midwest region for the Metropolitan Opera Company's auditions. Along with several others, I was connected with politics and concerned about social issues.

My concerns had grown out of volunteer work three mornings a week at the Capitol Community Center nursery school. Reading the case histories of the school's students, I had learned how difficult it was for poor people of all ethnic backgrounds to bring up their children. Parents needed child-care centers, where they could safely leave their children while they worked, and they needed medical care close to where they lived. I became a proponent of early childhood education, for it was through education that many immigrants had joined the mainstream of American society. Even more important, I saw for the first time the cost of urban redevelopment on people. I witnessed the hurt and confusion suffered by long-time residents who had been displaced, and by low-income groups for whom there were limited relocation possibilities because of the city's lack of low-cost housing. Incensed by the inhumanity of the relocation process, I asked the center staff what could be done to relieve the situation. They agreed with

my assessment of the problem, but told me they were simply
pawns in a policy issue decided by political higher-ups. Who
and where those higher-ups were, was a puzzle that would
take me time to solve.

The disparity between the economic plight of the people
who lived near the center and the living standard of our
social and economic group tested my sense of fairness. I
appeased my conscience and consoled myself with the fact
that I was learning about the plight of the underprivileged.
My knowledge of how public policy was formulated and
changed was in the embryonic stage. On a trip to Sweden (I
accompanied the U.S. Olympic hockey team that Rob managed in 1952), I visited several social agencies and was
fascinated by how another political culture solved its social
problems: the government funded the social agencies. Their
nursery schools for the poor put my school to shame. The
classrooms were modern and had the latest toys and educational equipment. The equally well equipped and comfortable
homes for unwed mothers were quite something. Since there
was no obvious social stigma attached to out-of-wedlock
births, it was as if sin had been made attractive. Because the
rural Republicans in Dakota County frowned on government
welfare handouts, I, an emerging Republican worker, did not
mention how Sweden solved its social concerns. Instead, I
integrated my new knowledge into the learning I was doing
about other local issues.

Another venture that augmented my political growth was
serving as a discussion leader for the Republican Workshop.
It frustrated me that some people did not view politics as
their civic duty. In early 1950, at Kay Harmon's home, women
from the Hennepin County Republican Workshop presented
their political education program called "Education for Action." I latched onto the program immediately, becoming a

discussion group leader for the Ramsey-Washington-Dakota County Workshop that was formed after the meeting at Kay's house.

The workshop course of four meetings, usually held in a home and led by a discussion leader, was an abbreviated study of political activism. Normally, the members of the group were strangers, but talking to people came naturally to me. I assumed that people liked me until it became obvious that we were at swords' points. When I asked the opening question of the first session, "What is your opinion of politics?" the most common response was negative: it was a corrupt business run by greedy politicians. Others never thought about politics, had too much else to do, or believed their one vote would not make any difference. I clearly remember leaning forward in my chair and trying to arouse interest in politics among this lethargic group. I energetically used statistics to prove how many elections had been won by just a few votes. With these tactics, I hoped to engage the participants in party work and to entice them to become members of the workshop. I was ecstatic when I found two or three people who responded to my message. If I had no successes, I would drive home exhausted from my futile efforts.

On the other hand, I progressed up the organizational ladder of the Republican Party. By 1952, I had risen from precinct work to district chairwoman, and finally to county chairwoman, when I was appointed to succeed Rose Schonning, the incumbent, who had resigned after being appointed postmistress of Farmington. Achieving my goal because of political patronage — a facet of the "spoils system" — strained my political idealism. Postmasterships, of course, were a political plum. In a democracy, people should work in politics for the good of the country. I knew how hard Rose, a farmwife, had labored for the party, and in the tradition of political payoff, she was more deserving than most, particularly because she was a woman.

Rose was also a shrewd politician. At conventions, I noticed early on that she did not join the large group of women who sat waiting for the proceedings to begin. She joined the men at the back of the hall who fraternized with elected officials, exchanged political gossip, or listened to potential candidates for office. Here was where the dance for political power took place. I soon circulated among that group.

In my new capacity, I had contact with Republican women all over the county. One of my favorite township chairwomen was Christina Huddleston, who ran a small country store in Lakeville. Of Dutch heritage, Christina had an ample figure, an apple-cheeked face, and hair she wore in a braid wound around her head. One day, I arrived to get her advice about a political caravan that I was organizing to get out the vote for Eisenhower and the other Republican candidates before the November election. I asked her for the names of some men. "Ach," she replied, "don't count on the men. The women do all the work. The men only want the titles." Yes, the women performed all the detail work, but I had to give my chairman, Walter Klaus, high marks for working hard and for getting farmers to meetings. I had no wish to alienate the male Republicans. In fact, I was most cordial at functions, for they gave the money to run campaigns. Women did not open their pocketbooks because political giving was still a male domain. I had become sufficiently astute to know that to win elections, the party could not alienate any potential group of voters.

Just as patronage tested my idealism, so did the job of collecting money for the party. I did not mind asking for funds. What galled me was discovering that Republican businessmen, along with the big corporations, gave to both sides of the aisle. Like most other women, I was still untutored in how money played into political lobbying, how businesses wanted access to both parties to protect themselves, for instance, against unfavorable tax legislation.

Dakota County had not gone Republican in a national election since 1928. In 1952, after looking at early canvass results, the county organization optimistically predicted a victory for the party. Despite our caravans of decorated cars and trucks through both the north and south sections of the county, and intense canvassing and telephoning to get out the vote, Eisenhower lost the county by nineteen votes.

Four years later it was a different story. Eisenhower carried the county, and Walter Klaus was elected to the state legislature. In between, I had been elected an alternate delegate from the Second Congressional District to the Republican National Convention in San Francisco. There were no challengers to President Eisenhower's renomination in 1956. Consequently, the district fight over delegates and alternate positions was eliminated, and following custom the delegates were divided equally between male and female. Even though I had been assured support from the delegates, until the final vote was recorded, I was afraid my candidacy would be contested. A progressive on social issues, a fiscal moderate who was not opposed to all taxation, and a suburbanite, I was not representative of my conservative, rural district. The specter of privilege was a constant factor in my relations with rural colleagues. I always refrained from mentioning my eastern upbringing. When it inadvertently came up, invariably someone commented, "Oh, that explains your accent. I knew you weren't a Minnesotan, but wondered where you came from." In my mind the election represented a big political achieve-

ment. Only Harold Stassen's ill-founded campaign to dump
Richard Nixon as Eisenhower's running mate kept the convention in San Francisco from being a total bore.

Back home, my position in the county party structure
had become much stronger. Bill Mears, the new county chairman (Klaus had resigned to run for legislative office), was a
businessman. He had little time to run a county political
party or political campaigns, leaving the job to me. Sensing
an Eisenhower win and euphoric at the chance to lead a campaign, I devoted all my energies the summer and fall of 1956
to the election. After eight years of politics, my organizational
skills were now well sharpened. More effective as a speaker, I
knew when to be humorous with political anecdotes and
when to press for workers. I usually planted two or three
women and men at meetings who seconded my pleas to get
out the vote. We celebrated our victory at a surprise party for
Walter Klaus in my home. In the basement playroom, which
was decorated with "Klaus in the House" signs and Ike bal-
loons, we boisterously congratulated Walter and each other.

After the election, I decided in early 1957 to serve out my
term as county chairwoman and not run in 1958. At first,
working for the party was invigorating. Although politics had
definitely provided me with a measure of an independent life,
eventually the endless meetings dragged and became lacklus-
ter. The gulf between my political stands and those of other
Republicans in the district widened: they were interested in
crop subsidies and property taxes, issues that I recognized
affected their livelihood. I yearned to talk about broader
social issues. And finally, I had achieved my personal goal of
being a county chairwoman. I was not conscious, however,
that achieving the goal was a milestone in my life. A decade
of political activity had honed my ability to lead. Appear-
ances before political groups had matured me into a

self-assured woman who welcomed the challenge of political persuasion, an art that carried into the civil rights and women's movements. Also, the knowledge I had acquired about how to function within a political structure was to be a major factor in my future effectiveness as a feminist.

During that same period, Rob's drinking had increased substantially. I sometimes came home late from political meetings and found him out like a light in his chair, and I knew that he had spent the evening imbibing. At parties the burden of observing him quietly have one drink after another was eased only by the knowledge that he realized he was drinking too much. He never seemed to have had too much, and as a result his drinking was not apparent to either the family or our friends. I didn't drink and consequently hadn't a clue about how liquor affected one. I advised him to cut down on his intake. We had endless conversations about the problem, and then Rob would drink only wine for long periods and beer for other lengths of time. That wasn't the answer, for I discovered that with a beer he would have a whiskey chaser. Yet, I never discussed my concerns with anyone. I had such faith that between us we would find a solution because Rob recognized he drank to excess.

My faith was almost gone, however, when this on-again, off-again hard liquor routine reached a climax in March 1957. I went to New York to be with Mother for a week. Rob promised to stay on the wagon while I was away. When he told me the evening I returned that he had been drinking, I walked out of the library and said I was going to drive Lillian home. I had to get out of the house before I exploded. I dropped Lillian off at her South St. Paul home, and driving back in the car, I screamed out questions: What was I going to do? Should I threaten to ask him to leave the house? Was it worth it to break up the family? What about my life alone without him? What about divorce? How would I earn money? Selling clothes? God forbid! Go back to college and get my teaching degree? Exhausted, I went to bed when I got home, got up the next morning, and took the children to school without saying a word to my husband. Rob and I were so sensitive to each other's feelings, there was no need to say that I had had enough.

Several days later, Rob returned home in the evening to say he had joined Alcoholics Anonymous. I wept in his arms.

We left shortly afterward on a trip to Asia. It would be very different from our trips to Europe, where we spent most of our time driving from one locale to another, armed with numerous guidebooks. In this way, we had traveled through England, France, Italy, Scotland, Spain, and West Germany. We were inveterate tourists. It was almost as if we were drugged by the desire to see every church, town hall, and corner shrine, to eat in every small, cheap, offbeat restaurant, and to spend the night in European inns loaded with local color. Because of letters of introduction from various organizations, such as the American Red Cross (Rob was on the national board), CBS, and the American Hockey Association, we were royally feted in Japan, Taiwan, Hong Kong, and the Philippines. A correspondent from each of the CBS bureaus was assigned to us for the four to ten days we spent in each country. They provided us with a golden opportunity to learn about the economic, social, and religious makeup of each place.

The trip brought to a close our first ten years in St. Paul. I came home invigorated by the vitality of the East, much more informed about Asia, and knowing that vacations with my husband were still an enriching part of my life. The greatest reward was that Rob had never gone off the wagon. But

A formal dinner in Japan with Red Cross representatives, 1957

the trip had lasted only a month. What assurance did I have that he would remain a member of AA?

The next six months were a restless time for me. Having quit politics, which had provided me with a sense of independent activity, I did not relish the prospect of being only a wife and mother, an appendage to family life. Measuring my world by the traditional standards applied to an upper-class suburban wife with an executive husband and financial security, I scored well. I was appreciated and loved. Life at times was frenetic but satisfying as I jumped from political activities to social service board meetings to Women's Institute work and family activities. I was not angry with my privileged life. What nagged at me was the question of Rob's drinking: What if he started again? What safety net did I have? How would I continue to live in the lifestyle to which I had become accustomed? I had an independence gene inherited from and nourished by my mother. She advised young married women to scrimp and save to establish a rainy-day bank account in their own names, without informing their husbands. Her sales force at Kathleen's included some upper-class women who had been left high and dry after divorce. She had seen what happened to women who had neither money nor marketable skills. I lacked a skill to give me a steady income.

Despite the closeness between Rob and me, I did not talk with him about my situation if he went back to drinking. That would display a lack of support and a lack of confidence in his ability to stay with AA. While I wrestled with my confusion, Rob did hear me say, every so often, "Now that I am not going to continue as county chairwoman, I think I will go to the U and get my teaching degree."

At Duluth State Teachers College I had taken courses that were applicable toward a teaching degree. I figured that a year or a year and a half was needed to fulfill the remaining requirements, a sufficient length of time to ascertain Rob's commitment to AA and for me to focus on my future. I enrolled at the University of Minnesota for spring quarter of 1958.

CHAPTER 3

≈

Working for Equal Rights

Today the University of Minnesota is a large urban institution with about sixty-five thousand students. When I enrolled in the spring of 1958, about thirty-six thousand students attended. I registered as an adult special student and petitioned to have all my credits from Smith and Duluth State Teachers College accepted toward the teaching degree—a bachelor of science in secondary school education—that I intended to earn. For the next year and a half, I attended classes that prepared me to become a teacher.

Shortly before the end of winter quarter in 1959, Edith West, my adviser, asked if she could recommend me for a position in the suburban Hopkins school system for the following fall. Thrown off guard by the unexpected possibility of a teaching position, I quickly replied that I would be unable to apply for a fall position. Because of family responsibilities, I hastened to explain, I wouldn't be able to complete all my course work that spring and expected to finish student teaching in the fall. I thanked her profusely for thinking of me and retreated as quickly as possible from her office. Dr. West's offer had clearly unnerved me. Why was I loath to make the decision to teach? The academic year had been particularly rewarding: my persona was that of a student, not a wife of an executive or mother of three children. Dr. West certainly thought of me as a future teacher; otherwise she would not have apprised me of a job opportunity. Classmates regarded me as a fellow undergraduate who did well in class, an achievement based solely on my ability. The truth was, I did not want my academic career to end. Blessed with excellent health and no financial constraints, I wanted the luxury of being a student to continue. It was easy for me to put the decision off until the fall, justifying the action (to myself, as well as to my adviser) by citing the number of family commitments I had on my plate.

During Easter vacation in 1959, Chou-Chou and I visited boarding schools. Rob and I agreed that if the children were amenable, the experience of going away to school would be a valuable one for them. I wanted our daughter to attend a school similar to Brearley and have the experience of being in the East. Our most successful interview was with Miss Spear, the head of Shipley School, which had both day and boarding students and an academic program similar to Brearley's. She was a warm, intelligent person who empathized with a young girl from Minnesota venturing out on her own, as it were. Located on the Main Line in Bryn Mawr, Pennsylvania, Shipley was an easy commute to New York City. Rob and I were pleased when the letter of acceptance arrived for Chou to enter in the fall of 1959.

Our family and Mother plus my brother Peter spent most of the intervening time traveling in the Middle East and Europe. My personal treasure from the trip was the knowledge I acquired about Arab women. On the drive from Beirut to Damascus, I saw that the men rode in donkey-pulled carts, surrounded by walking women and children. The women, dressed in chadors, carried bundles of grain or firewood on their heads. Along the road any arable land was cultivated by the women. Women appeared to be little more than beasts of burden and tillers of the soil.

In Damascus, we visited a Palestinian refugee camp. The poverty was overwhelming and the odor of urine pervasive;

dust and dirt swirled around in the breeze. Girls and women peered out from mud hovels at us, the rich Americans. In a clearing, the women sat on their haunches, heads drawn together in a black circle, still as mice when we passed, not wanting — or unable — to acknowledge us. Mother called them the black crows. It was amazing to me that, so often, all we saw of these women was their eyes and that their composure and carriage made them seem invisible.

I yearned to communicate with the women in the old sections of Cairo whose eyes scrutinized us from behind black veils. Along the narrow streets, some women sat on low chairs and peeled vegetables. It would have been a perfect moment to open a conversation, if language had not been a barrier. In open spaces, the women crouched in a circle, a custom that appeared natural to many Arab women. The black circle later became my metaphor when I explained to my friends how women were treated in that part of the world: they were without light, under a cloud, in a dark hole, ignored and looked on by the men as property without human rights.

The black circle haunted me as we traveled from Egypt and Greece to the capitals of Western Europe. While Mother, Chou, and I visited fashion houses in Rome and Paris, I contrasted the black garments worn by the women we had seen with the fabulous colors the haute couture models were showing to prospective buyers. In my view, the lives of Western women were light-years ahead of those of Arab women. What if I had been born there rather than in my world? The year was 1959 and the women's movement had not yet emerged; equal rights and gender equity were not yet part of my vocabulary. Even without a movement to validate my sense of the Arab woman's situation, I found myself thinking, gratefully, "There but for the grace of God go I."

Back home in Minnesota, preparing for Chou's departure for boarding school, I knew that my involvement in my daughter's life was embarking on a new path. No longer would she be at the dinner table chatting about her day's activities. In mid-September, our final words, after kisses and hugs at the airport gate, were, "Be sure and call us tonight." I missed my daughter enormously and worried that sending her to boarding school might not have been the right decision. After several phone calls and letters assuring us that she had adjusted and was happy, it seemed that Chou would be just fine, and although I still missed her, I stopped worrying. My life as a student, wife, and mother easily resumed its rhythm.

In the fall, Edith West suggested several suburban high schools to which she would be glad to recommend me, forcing me to come to grips again with my future. Rob had been a member of AA for two years, and confident of his sobriety, I had no valid need to work. I was faced with a different quandary. I'd had great success at practice teaching. My excellent grades echoed my love of teaching, making it difficult to deny that teaching was a logical profession to enter. Here was my chance to have a life of my own, yet I did not jump at the opportunity. Why?

I struggled with the stress it would cause were I to abandon the social mores a woman of my privileged status was expected to uphold. How would the children react to a working mother who left five mornings a week to teach? No mother among their friends — or mine — worked. Could I ensure that I had help in the house? I certainly did not need a job to earn money. Would I take a teaching position away from someone whose livelihood depended on the salary? I was happily married with three normal, happy children. I wrestled with my dilemma without consulting Rob because I wanted the decision to be mine — with no one else's influ-

ence. To solve my predicament, I chose the safest solution
available to a woman of my era: I got pregnant.

I think now that, if the women's movement had been in full
swing, giving women the impetus and support to break out
on their own, my analysis of my position might have been
different. But at that point in my life, I simply didn't have the
audacity to jump outside the mainstream of my social peers,
nor did I have the need. Early on, Rob and I had planned to
have four children. Now seemed the appropriate time to add
to our family. Later, in the 1970s, I discovered other women
who had faced the same dilemma and had chosen motherhood, thereby winning the approbation of society. Having
made that commitment, I didn't brood about it or rail against
society. I comprehended well the circumstances of my privileged position and wanted to remain within that framework.
I didn't regret my decision, and I learned from the experience,
an addition to the stored inventory that influenced me along
my way to being a feminist.

Fortunately, an opportunity had arisen that helped redirect my energy to an all-absorbing new focus — the civil rights
movement. Rob and I had followed the emergence of the civil
rights struggle in the South, beginning in December 1955
with Rosa Parks's refusal to give up her bus seat to a white
man in Montgomery, Alabama. I applauded Mrs. Parks's
courage; segregation laws conflicted with my sense that all
races should be treated equally. We watched on television the
weekly developments of the boycott by blacks of the Montgomery Bus Company, and saw the rise of Martin Luther
King Jr. as the new leader. It was a time of ferment in the
South, but Montgomery and the Southern Christian Leadership Conference were a long way from Minnesota. Stirred up
by the media, I began searching for how I, a suburbanite and

a member of the establishment, could find work in an organization devoted to civil rights, an issue I deemed of vital
importance to my country's future. A timely invitation came
in 1957 to join the Urban League's board of directors from
Jean and Carl Schuneman, a well-known couple in St. Paul
(Carl was the owner and president of Schuneman's department store). They were about to resign from the board, and
the nominating committee had asked them to find another
couple to take their places.

The Urban League, founded in St. Paul in 1923, was an
interracial organization. Its purpose was to improve living
and working conditions for blacks and to inform the white
community about the problems facing blacks in St. Paul, the
majority of whom lived in an area known as Selby-Dale. The
Urban League was, and still is, funded by the United Way,
which in 1958 was called the Community Chest. The league
staff acted as the link between blacks and social agencies in
St. Paul and worked to open up the job market to them. The
board was composed of about an equal number of blacks
and whites from various economic backgrounds.

At our first meeting, Rob and I were curious to know
how the board functioned to promote understanding between
the races. We met over dinner in the basement of the YWCA
on Fifth Street in downtown St. Paul. During dinner I was
conscious that I had never sat and "broken bread" at the
same table with black people. Looking around, I saw a
tableau of both black and white faces, sharing food and
engrossed in amiable conversation — such a stark contrast to
the confrontational events reported on the television. I
wanted to believe that our gathering predicted harmonious
race relations. After several dinners, we discovered that the
overriding issue facing the board was the proposed construction of I-94 in the Selby-Dale area — specifically how the

freeway would affect the people living on Rondo and St. Anthony Streets. Father Denzil Carty, the pastor of St. Philip's Episcopal Church and the chair of the Urban League board, and the Reverend Floyd Massey, a board member, reported on their appearance before the St. Paul City Council and the state highway department's hearings held in the community. Supported by the board's vote, they had strongly opposed the interstate going through their community. That fight was lost, but later, they, the Urban League, and other members of the community won the battle to have the highway depressed rather than raised through St. Paul.

Rob and I quickly learned of other challenges facing St. Paul's black population. To begin with, I had naively thought that the residents whose homes were to be purchased by the highway department would welcome the opportunity to sell and move to better areas of the city. Instead, the reality was that because of housing discrimination, the dislocated families' only option was to buy homes that were left behind by whites fleeing the Selby-Dale area. The real estate agents engineered the white flight; they encouraged whites to put up their homes for sale to blacks.

As board members — particularly the whites — recognized more fully the issues facing the community, the members debated during the next several years the role of the Urban League, particularly in relation to the Selby-Dale area. The league was a social agency whose board set policy to be implemented by the staff. The debate centered on how active the board should be in the work of the organization. I agreed with board members who wanted the agency and board to be more connected to the community, and was disappointed when in 1961 the league offices moved downtown to the new YWCA building on Kellogg Boulevard, instead of to the Selby-Dale area.

Underlying my commitment to the advancement of equal opportunity was the idealistic philosophy that good educations led to good jobs, which in turn provided educated blacks with the means to buy houses in white neighborhoods. I thought that ethnic groups living in integrated areas would intermarry, intermarriage being a step toward total integration of our society. After all, the women who toiled in Kathleen, Inc.'s workroom did so to provide their children a good education, which moved them up the social and economic ladder. What I did not realize was that I understood so little about the realities of the black experience, and failed to see what a barrier skin color was to upward mobility.

I steamed ahead for the next four years (1961–1965), attending Urban League board meetings and learning about the community from meetings on employment, education, and housing. Each meeting's discussion energized us to explore possibilities to forge new areas of harmony between the races and further integration. The most important issue to surface was the emerging "de facto" segregation taking place in Maxfield and McKinley elementary schools. The forecast that discrimination in housing would be caused by the freeway had come to pass: whites were selling their homes to blacks, the result of which was fewer white students in the schools. In its 1961 session, the state legislature passed the Fair Housing Law, which prohibited discrimination on the part of real estate agents, as a way to stop white flight. The media reported daily on the activities of the national civil rights movement, which strengthened my dedication to working for equal rights.

The majority of our social friends, however, were not as dedicated to the movement. If the subject arose, I answered questions but carefully avoided adversarial situations. I had been badly unnerved by an incident that took place in the fall of 1962. At a Saturday luncheon, I sat next to Norm Van Brocklin, coach of the Vikings football team. The talk centered on Tommy Mason, a white running back of slight build who was prone to injuries. Stories in the sports pages had talked of the Vikings getting a black running back who was stronger physically. I inserted this idea into the conversation and immediately Van Brocklin asked very aggressively, "And whom do you suggest we hire?" I realized I was being baited and turned to the man on my left to ask him who he thought was a possibility. The conversation drifted on about running backs and I took a backseat. At the end of lunch, as I rose to leave, Van Brocklin put his arm around my shoulders and said in front of everyone, "Here's our nigger lover." Inwardly, I recoiled, but I kept my cool, immediately said good-bye — looking Van Brocklin straight in the eye — found Rob, and left. In the car going home, I asked Rob if he thought Van Brocklin would have said that to a man. He answered no. If I had been a man, I might have hit Van Brocklin, but I was a woman who had been taught not to lower my standards, even when challenged. My only recourse was to be polite and leave. During the ride I also mentioned that Van Brocklin had spoken derogatorily about several black running backs, belittling them even though they were known as good football players, and that his remarks had angered me.

Van Brocklin failed to intimidate me, however. His remarks, in fact, drove me to even more activity, and I took a greater interest in school desegregation. I joined Parents for Integrated Education (PIE), an organization started by women in 1964. Patty Bratnober, the first president of PIE, asked why white parents in the Highland Park section of St. Paul could not act as sponsors of black students from Selby-Dale, enabling them to attend classes in that school district. She assembled a group of like-minded people, and PIE was

established. After the St. Paul school board endorsed open
enrollment on April 25, 1965, the group sprang into action.
Open enrollment meant that if there were empty spaces in a
classroom, the space could be filled by a student from outside
that particular school's district.

The Urban League Guild, a group of black and white
women of which I was a member and an affiliate of the
Urban League, arranged coffee parties to make PIE members
available to black parents who were interested in open enrollment. In the middle of August, with several other women, I
went door to door in the Selby-Dale community, visiting
homes and informing black parents about the program. Our
canvassing took place during the six days of the Watts riots in
Los Angeles, which were covered extensively on television. In
contrast with the rampant fear and violence in California, I
felt perfectly safe sitting in people's living rooms discussing
PIE and its objectives. Seventy-three black students made use
of the program that first year.

At the beginning of my work with this organization, the
only woman I knew was Patty Bratnober. My previous personal contact with the black women in their own community
(most of the blacks on the Urban League board were men)
had been minimal, and many of the other white women were
from the Jewish community in Highland Park; I might not
have met them had it not been for PIE. Bonded by our common cause, our relationships evolved into a smooth pattern
of give-and-take. I was grateful to at last come to know a
group of black people with whom I could talk on an informal
basis. Sometimes during our conversations the black women
pointed out a remark that might be construed as racist. Those
of us who considered ourselves "in" with the civil rights movement learned how important the use of language was in
recognizing the diversity that existed between the races. But

there were obvious similarities, too. Both races were economically divided; the blacks who lived south of Rondo were
less well off than those north of the street. Both blacks' and
whites' lives centered, not only religiously, but also socially,
on their churches, and both had clubs that served a variety
of social functions.

The women's Cameo Club, for example, sponsored an
annual ball at which members' debutante daughters were presented. Lillian Ballenger, whom I knew from the Urban
League, was president when she asked me to emcee the event
in the early 1960s. It was held in the ballroom of the Cal-
houn Beach Club in Minneapolis. I read each young woman's
name as she descended the balcony stairs; her escort then
greeted her and led her to the end of the ballroom. After all
the debutantes were introduced, I and a very handsome, tall
black man, the husband of a committee member, led off the
dancing. It was a totally enjoyable evening. I was taken aback
several days later when a woman, who didn't identify herself,
called and upbraided me for participating in a social function
with blacks. She had read about the affair in the newspaper,
she said, and stated that a woman of my economic and social
status should not demean herself by associating with "nig-
gers." I listened silently, boiling with rage. I hung up without
saying a word, relieved that I had not exploded in anger,
revealing emotions — and opinions — that would not have
changed her mind. I could have told her, with some satisfaction, that the Cameo Club event was the first debutante
party — either black or white — to which I had been invited
since I'd moved to St. Paul, and that I had had a good time.

Functioning in the civil rights movement in St. Paul and living in the suburbs of Dakota County made me acutely aware
that few Minnesotans knew or cared about the civil rights

laws passed by the state legislature and the U.S. Congress. Despite media coverage, the people with whom I associated had no knowledge of the 1961 Fair Housing Law and the Civil Rights Act of 1964, nor were many taking responsibility for initiating integration in their own neighborhoods. This point came home to me in a conversation with three members of the Catholic Interracial Council after we gave a panel presentation (I was chair of the speakers' bureau) at a new suburban Catholic parish. In the car en route home, we analyzed why our message, exhorting Christian responsibility in regard to integration, had fallen so far short. We concluded that people saw integration in the workplace as a threat to their jobs; similarly, they viewed housing integration as a threat to the value of their new homes, which they had bought after years of scrimping and saving to get out of the inner-city school system. We, on the other hand, were a group of established suburbanites who preached Christian duty but whose livelihoods were not necessarily threatened by integration. I recall saying that we were not alone in our efforts, that other people in our economic and social stratum had successfully carried the message of integration. As an example, I named Eleanor Roosevelt, just as I was let off at my home.

I have no idea what effect my example had on my companions, but it profoundly affected me. I wrestled with my identification of being a white, suburban woman who interfered in areas where she did not belong. Many blacks were often suspicious of my commitment to civil rights and did not always trust me. Spontaneously, Eleanor Roosevelt emerged as a role model, someone for me to emulate. I had secretly admired her during my school years, despite the criticism from my mother's Republican friends about her 1930s newspaper column, "My Day." In the face of enormous disapproval

Mrs. Roosevelt had dedicated her life to social justice and equality. My social, economic, and political base did not compare with hers; nonetheless, as a Republican, a woman whose husband's position was not threatened by integration, and a Christian, I had as equal an opportunity to effect social justice reform.

That heady optimism was soon tempered by the rise of Black Power. From my political work, I understood the desire to develop an identity with political power based on one's own culture. Many immigrant groups had formed such power bases. I saw the Black Power movement running parallel with the civil rights coalition of blacks and whites, and believed it was another avenue through which integration would be fostered. Politically, Black Power was centered in the Democratic Party. The majority of people with whom I worked were Democrats who often chided me about my affiliation with the Republican Party. When asked to join the Democrats, I declined, knowing that the Democrats were well supplied with civil rights supporters. I also noted that not all Republicans were against equal opportunity: my congressman, Al Quie, had voted for the Civil Rights Act of 1964. I would stay in the party and work with sympathetic members to spread the message of equal rights. Nevertheless, my Republican connection isolated me politically from the Black Power movement, and I felt myself being eased out, the black-white coalition of which I was a part no longer the dominant force in integration.

The majority of the Urban League continued to believe that the league, a social agency, should not embroil itself in the Black Power movement. From my perspective, after Sam Jones left in August 1966 and Larry Borom became director, the organization became more highly politicized. By 1968, I had served on the board for ten years and did not run for reelection. I believed as strongly as ever in the civil rights movement, but I had no desire to get caught up in an acrimonious debate about the role of the Urban League.

I continued my work elsewhere and joined the board of PIE. With five other women, I initiated the renovation of Oxford Playground in Selby-Dale. In the summer of 1967, an article had appeared in the newspaper detailing the disbursements of the Capitol Improvement Budget (CIB) for the city of St. Paul, including expenditures for pool construction in the playgrounds. I could not believe it when I saw that no funds had been allocated for a pool at Oxford Playground, which was located in a section of St. Paul that needed it the most. At a chance meeting with Patty Bratnober at the Somerset Country Club, I enlisted her aid in forming a committee of black and white women to investigate the possibility of getting funds for Oxford. Eloise Adams, Billie Carter, and Augusta Schroeder, black women leaders in the community, plus Patty Bratnober, Marie Perry, and I, formed a committee that became referred to as "those women." We claimed the label after a meeting with city officials who referred to us as "those women" who had no business meddling in city affairs. Our group went to see Sam Morgan, an old friend, who chaired the CIB committee. He was most cordial, but he told us that decisions about parks and recreation were made in Commissioner Vic Tedesco's office. Tedesco, however, had no money to build a pool at Oxford. We knew Tedesco, a politician, would not consider taking money from any other playground, no matter how much pressure we exerted. Undaunted by the negative answers from city hall, we began to hold periodic meetings at the Loft, a teen center at Laurel and Selby Avenues. After we explored many options, we found money for our project from Model Cities, a new federally funded program targeting the inner cities. The leaders of the black community, skeptical at first about our plan for a pool at Oxford, joined us when they realized there might be monies to build it. We revised our project goals, deciding to get funds for a large recreational center first and then build a pool.

By the summer of 1969, sufficient funds from Model Cities had been allocated to build the center. At the groundbreaking ceremony, Eloise Adams spoke, representing "those women." A teenage Dave Winfield, who was later to become a famous baseball player, spoke on behalf of the youth who used Oxford. It was ironic that Mayor Tom Byrne and Commissioner Tedesco, both of whom had fought us all the way, took credit when they shoveled a bit of dirt to symbolize the opening, while Augusta, Billie, and I stood in the audience.

Deeply engaged as I was in the civil rights movement, it was impossible for me not to know what was transpiring in the debate over women's rights. In fact, Whitney Young, the president of the national Urban League, at a lunch in late 1967 alerted me in graphic terms that the real revolution in this country would happen when the white woman realized how she had been "screwed" by the white man. Even though I had witnessed white male politicians taking credit for women's work, I did not harbor such animosity. My involvement in civil rights had satisfied my yearning to be identified on my own terms. I had organized meetings and conferences in concert with blacks and whites, men and women, around integration, one of the dominant and controversial issues of the 1960s. At Maxfield School I taught reading to black children in the first and second grades. Many of them "latchkey" girls and boys, the students had reading problems similar to those of white youngsters from the same socioeconomic backgrounds. To relieve the monotony of Dick and Jane books, the kids and I discussed various topics, their favorite being *Star Trek*. Lively talk ensued, laced with many black colloquialisms that had to be explained to me. The knowledge that I acquired from my experiences with race relations was not found in books; it was *lived* experience.

My activities on behalf of civil rights had not gone unnoticed by the Republican Party. Governor Harold LeVander asked me to serve on the state Board of Human Rights in October 1969, and I accepted immediately. It was an opportunity to participate in forming public policy in the area of civil and human rights with a state agency, and I simply could not pass it up.

Created in 1967, the state board was an advisory body that recommended programs and policies to the Department of Human Rights and also acted as an appeal board. Despite ten years' experience and intense interest in civil rights, I had difficulty finding my niche on the board. I came from a suburban district that had few minority residents, and even though the department was flooded with race and sex discrimination cases, none came from my area. The one appeal panel on which I served dealt with sex discrimination in a bakery. The case involved a female baker who was paid less than the male bakers for the same hours of work. After reading the formal charge, I, along with the other two members of the panel — both of whom were men — decided that the woman should be paid the same wages as her male counterparts. It gratified me that the two men agreed that women should have equal pay. I had assumed the first appeal case on which I served would deal with race, because all of my civil rights work to that point had dealt with racial issues. Amazingly, in 1971, the largest block of people using the department's services were women filing sex discrimination cases in employment, an indication that the emerging women's movement was having an impact on the economic status of women.

An integral function of the department was to establish in cities statewide human rights commissions that were to act as vehicles for social change. The six commissions set up in Dakota County were little more than paper organizations giving lip service to civil rights. Several cities invited me to come and discuss the role that their commission was expected to play. When I informed the department that I had accepted these invitations, I was quickly told that a staff person must accompany me and that none was available to do so. My immediate reaction was that the staff did not trust my ability to define the function of a commission and that commissions in the rural and suburban areas were less important than those in the large cities. In fairness, the staff was saddled with an enormous workload, but the abruptness of their response dampened my spirits. Where they really needed my assistance, they said, was lobbying legislators in Dakota County to get them to vote for civil rights legislation.

My sensitivity to discrimination was personally heightened by the failure of the 1971 legislative session to pass a bill that added protection from discrimination on the basis of sex in housing, education, public accommodations, and public services. The Department of Human Rights initiated the legislation, and I lobbied for it. The 1955 antidiscrimination bill had not included sex among its classifications, and the fact that sixteen years later women were still excluded from protection against discrimination in those areas was an absolute affront. It shocked me to realize that if I wanted to buy a house, I might suffer discrimination in the process and have no legal recourse. I now understood more fully what blacks experienced when they tried to move out of the ghetto.

When my term on the state Board of Human Rights ended in January 1972, I did not seek reappointment, and after fifteen years in the civil rights movement, my active

involvement with race relations came to an end. With the
passage of national and state civil rights legislation, I trusted
that the laws would be implemented and enforced with all
deliberate speed. Instead, roadblocks appeared at every turn.
Blacks had reacted by becoming more militant, forming the
Black Power movement. Paralleling that was "white backlash." What I knew was that I had been able to work
cooperatively in the Selby-Dale area with men and women,
blacks and whites, and that we shared the same goals. Things
had changed. At the end of my two years on the Board of
Human Rights I sensed the same "easing out" I had experienced in my final year in the Urban League. My being a white
woman who lived in the suburbs, had money, and was a
Republican married to a man in the media appeared to dis-
qualify me for any effectual work. A pragmatic person, I
wasted no time wondering what I could have done had I been
middle class or a Democrat. Other challenges had arisen, and
I chose to direct my energies toward them.

CHAPTER 4

⌒

CHAIRMAN, CHAIRWOMAN, CHAIR

Despite suggestions from friends who knew I had attended Smith College that I read *The Feminine Mystique* by Betty Friedan, a Smith graduate, I wasn't very interested. What I knew about the book came from reviews, which said that Friedan had written a well-documented portrayal of women's lives as emotionally empty. Friedan attributed women's lack of fulfillment to the "feminine mystique" that relegated them to being only wives and mothers — the desired role that society allotted to them. When the book was published in 1963, I had been married for twenty years, during which time I had combined a life as a wife and mother with an independent life of my own. Sustaining this existence had developed a creative force that enabled me to meet the vicissitudes of life and forge new directions. I had devised for myself a scheme of being attached to multiple activities. This gave me an option: if one course proved a failure, I could fall back on another. The author Mary Catherine Bateson refers to this as "improvisation." So far my course of action had served me well; even so, I had seen that women suffered discrimination. But as yet I had not personally faced discrimination to the extent that I became truly angry about women's place in society.

The consciousness-raising groups that became popular in the years following the publication of Friedan's book also did not appeal to me. I did not require sessions to analyze a life with which I was satisfied. Yet I knew that for many women these discussions were an opportunity to share experiences, develop a new perspective about their self-worth, and build a

network of friends who gave mutual support to each other —
a sisterhood. With their new way of thinking, these women
became, as I was to become, staunch supporters of women's
organizations.

Subscribing to the feminist definition of social, economic,
and political rights for women equal to men's, I supported the
Equal Rights Amendment (ERA). I joined the state chapter of
the National Organization for Women (NOW) in 1970, and
the Minnesota Women's Political Caucus (MWPC) in 1971,
because both organizations rallied support for the passage of
the ERA in Minnesota. Although I knew two of the Republican women on the MWPC's organizing committee — Emily
Ann Staples and Lu Stocker — I was not drawn to participate
because my political base was in Dakota County. There the
Republican Party, in the early 1970s, became more and more
conservative. A majority of the Dakota County Republican
women did not support the ERA. Phyllis Schlafly, the national
chair of Stop ERA, found fertile ground among these conservative women to plant her anti-ERA message. Knowing the
political climate in my county, I decided that to take an active
part in NOW or MWPC would have distanced me further
from my political base, which, at the time, was not an option
for me.

At the legislature, despite the conservatism of the Dakota
County Republicans, I lobbied representatives and senators
of both parties in my legislative districts to pass the ERA. The
1973 legislative session passed the amendment well before
the impact of the anti-ERA campaign was felt in Minnesota.
Jubilant Minnesota women — I among them — predicted the
amendment was well on its way to ratification. How wrong
we were.

My jubilation was bittersweet because in 1972 the
Republican Party had eliminated the ERA plank from the

state platform, an indication of the party's turn to the right. Nevertheless, I attended county conventions as a delegate from my precinct caucus. At these conventions, a sufficient number of convention delegates, in recognition of my past party work, elected me alternate delegate to district and state meetings.

The Republican Party's rightward swing forced me to confront my party allegiance. In 1964, I had refrained from working for Senator Barry Goldwater's presidential campaign because he was too conservative. In the 1968 presidential election, I was strongly tempted to vote for Hubert H. Humphrey. Vice President Humphrey was a native son, and I admired his leadership in the civil rights movement, both nationally and in Minnesota. I bothered Rob repeatedly with the question, "Why should I support Nixon?" He solved my predicament while we listened to the Republican National Convention on the car radio as we drove through Maine with Peter and Christopher. When it was announced that Nixon had chosen Spiro Agnew, the governor of Maryland, as his running mate, Rob exclaimed, "What the devil did he do that for?" I announced immediately, "That does it. I won't vote for Nixon. Who the heck is Agnew?" My declaration that I, a lifelong Republican, would not support a Republican presidential candidate so shook Rob that he made a deal with me: he promised to give up smoking if I voted for Nixon. I quickly reconsidered my decision. Over a long period of time, the doctor had urged Rob, who smoked two and one-half packs of cigarettes a day, to give up the habit. In addition, he had had several serious bouts with pneumonia. I agreed to the bargain: my husband's health was worth a vote for "tricky Dick."

Unlike some of my friends who became DFLers, I stayed with the Republican Party — it was where I had some politi-

cal strength. At every opportune moment, I pressured the
party to recognize the importance of women's issues because
it needed a percentage of the women's vote to win elections.
The women's movement had generated a head of steam, en-
couraging women to run for office. But the Democratic Party
had attracted far more women than the Republican Party. I
refused to change my political affiliation because when Republicans won elections, Republican women, advocates of
the women's agenda, had to be there to advance their cause.

Having made the decision to promote the women's
agenda within the political structure of the Republican Party,
I did not extend my participation any further. I was still too
involved with other social and civic causes. With a tendency
to look at the bright side, I construed being "eased out" of
the formal civil rights organizations as positive because I had
gained a wealth of knowledge about human relations. Moreover, I continued to pursue my commitment to civil rights by
working on the board of Parents for Integrated Education
(PIE), which opened the door to a new movement that dealt
with public educational policy. Shortly after PIE began promoting its busing program to further the integration of
schools, the board developed a program called ADAPT
(Appreciating Differences Among People and Things). The
program consisted of a series of lesson plans centered on children's self-conceptions, their perceptions of each other, and
their reactions to differences. Volunteers from PIE would lead
the children through the lesson plans for a class session. I did
not wholeheartedly embrace this program. Single class periods devoted to exploring differences seemed a contrived way
to instill an appreciation of diversity, but I kept silent because
I recognized that ADAPT was at least a step toward improving human relations in the classroom. My hope was that a
better method, such as incorporating the concept of diversity

within the total curriculum, specifically in textbooks, would become the norm.

Likewise, I learned to curb my tongue when busing for school integration in St. Paul was debated. The opposition to busing extolled the sanctity of the neighborhood school: children walked to the neighborhood school, neighborhood friendships were the basis of social life for children, and mothers were close to the school, in case they were needed. I had not attended a neighborhood school and had suffered no deprivation because of it. My experience was of students dressed in different uniforms, riding the New York subway to schools distant from their homes. They seemed happy swinging from the overhead straps as they talked a mile a minute about their activities. I tried to explain my perspective at a PIE meeting, and suddenly felt that the assembled group was looking at me thinking, "Poor dear, she doesn't know what she missed by not going to a neighborhood school!" After that reception, I refrained from referring to my youth.

By 1969, busing as a means of bringing about school integration had generated considerable controversy, and a backlash had developed. Another proposed solution, the tuition voucher, invited an equal amount of controversy. Under this system, a student would receive a certain sum of public money that would enable him or her to choose which school, public or private, to attend. To promote discussion about such alternatives in education, PIE, in cooperation with the St. Paul Public Schools, in November 1970 held a conference called "New Trends in Education." Jean Druker, another member of the PIE board, and I cochaired the meeting. As a first step we immediately rounded up eight other organizations to cosponsor the conference: the St. Paul School Committee, Model Cities, the St. Paul Council of Human Relations, the St. Paul PTA, Quality Integrated Edu-

cation for Everyone, the Coalition for Better Schools, the
League of Women Voters, and the St. Paul Urban Coalition.
The participating organizations planned a daylong program
consisting of four seminars that would run simultaneously in
the morning and then be repeated in the afternoon. The
speakers for the seminars came from Georgia, California,
Ohio, and New York. Dr. George P. Young, superintendent of
the St. Paul Public Schools, closed the conference with a summary of the day's discussions.

The larger-than-expected number of registrants proved
that it was a propitious time to hold the event. The turbu-
lence of the 1960s caused parents to question the public
school system and to seek alternatives to traditional methods
of teaching. The most appealing option to a particular group
of St. Paul parents was an open school, one of which was
already functioning in Mankato, Minnesota. In January
1971, I attended a public rally for open schools that was held
in the St. Paul Technical-Vocational Institute. Even though a
blizzard raged that night, more than six hundred people came
to hear Don Glines from Mankato speak about the open
school concept, which promoted individualized learning.
Glines gave such a glowing report about the success of this
new trend that I wanted to be a part of the movement. I
joined the list of volunteers who worked to have an open
school in place in St. Paul by the fall of 1971.

Considering the makeup of the St. Paul parents who were
seeking change, I was an anomaly: I had no children in the
public schools. My three older children had graduated from
private high schools, and Christopher, the youngest at age nine,
was at Breck School, a private school in Minneapolis. Chou
had graduated from Boston University, Robbie was a senior
at Hamilton College in upstate New York, and Peter had
been accepted at Brown University. They were the products

Our family in the late 1960s (left to right): Christopher, Rob, I, Kathleen, Peter, and Robbie

of private education who had come through the sixties with relatively few scars and had managed to avoid the drug culture. Because we had money, Rob and I had been able to choose where to send our children.

What was it, then, that drew me to the debate about education? First, I had a degree in education and had studied the various trends that shaped present teaching methods. I had learned firsthand of the many changes that had improved the educational system. Second, I came from a world in which change was constant. My father once said, as we walked around a barricade blocking a sidewalk, that New York City was never finished, that everything was always changing. Trolley cars were replaced by buses. The West Side Highway was built, and FDR Drive on the East Side followed. The retail business of New York relied on new fashions, new appliances, radios, televisions, new styles of furniture to keep customers streaming in. I had always liked the excitement of something new. Finally, I recognized that not all children learned in the same way and at the same pace. The system needed new methods to challenge and assist those students who were not succeeding with the traditional methods. Stories about innovative approaches to education were appearing in the media, and books like Jonathan Kozol's *Death at an Early Age,* about racism in education, were adding to the public debate. The question became, Why, in a democracy, should educational choice be limited to those who had money?

After the January rally, those parents who had expressed interest in establishing an open school by the fall of 1971 formed a group called Alternatives to spearhead the project. Through their untiring efforts — holding community meetings, seeking funds, and gaining school board approval — the St. Paul Open School opened its doors on schedule, to five hundred students in kindergarten through twelfth grade. There were one thousand students on the waiting list.

When the school opened at the renovated Univac Building on University Avenue, I was one of many people who volunteered to teach. An important part of the open school concept was to use community resources to supplement the teaching staff. I left Maxfield School, where I had been volunteering, because even though individual teachers expressed gratitude for my efforts from time to time, I did not feel part of the community. This may have been because I was the only volunteer, but at the Open School, it wasn't an issue. There were many of us, and we were included in curriculum planning. At my request, a variety of reading texts were provided in the reading center. Each child in the school had an individual study program, and I was listed as a reading teacher. In the reading center, I was sometimes the only teacher present. At Maxfield, I never had total responsibility for a child's

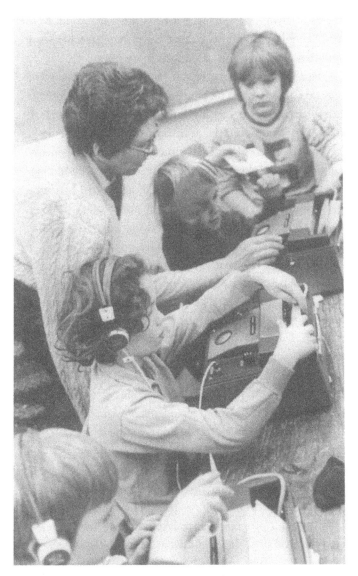

In the reading center at the St. Paul Open School

progress; I always complemented what the teacher did. At the
Open School I was, in many cases, the primary teacher working with a child, and that was much more rewarding.

Yet, the free-flowing character of the Open School sometimes taxed my faith in its philosophy that children would
learn when they were happily engaged in the educational
process. For many children, learning to read was difficult.
The slower students expended more time and mental energy
than did their quicker counterparts, learning short and long
vowels, consonants, and how to sound out words. Not surprisingly, the good readers came to the area regularly. At
times, I had to track down the poor readers and inveigle them
to come read. Some students responded positively; others
reacted so negatively that I regretted my impulsiveness.

By and large, however, I supported the philosophy
because I saw a diversified group of students who arrived at
school happy, self-confident, and ready to take part in the day's
activities. There were many more successes than failures, and
the failures simply fit better into the traditional method of
teaching. Parents were free to visit the Open School during
the school day, and parent-teacher meetings often took place
on an informal basis, with the students present.

There were many visitors besides parents who came to the
school. The first year, more than one thousand people visited
from Minnesota and other states. I was always enthusiastic
about talking with them and was pleased to answer their
questions about the reading program. Their interest made me
realize that our program was truly innovative, and that elevated the level of pride I felt in what I was doing.

While my venture into the development of state civil rights
public policy had been thwarted by the bureaucracy of the
Department of Human Rights, my involvement in the forma-

tion of local public policy was immensely successful. In the fall of 1969 I was asked by Mayor Don Huber to be a member of the first Parks and Recreation Commission in Mendota Heights. I was no stranger to the mayor or to the members of the city council.

From the early days of our residency in Mendota Heights, Rob and I read the *West St. Paul Booster,* which kept us abreast of local news. I loved the farmland, the wide-open spaces, the changes that the seasons wrought, and the sweep of the wind across the Mendota countryside. When the first snowstorm hit after we had moved into our house in the fall of 1947, I bundled up and stood outside on the hill, mesmerized by the snow swirling around me. I understood that development of the farmland was to come, but I hoped that the township would not be covered with rows of houses built side-by-side on a grid.

The Friendly Hills plat of the Weinzettel farm awakened the community to what future development might resemble. The three-member township board approved the plat, which divided the land into eleven-thousand-square-foot lots, each with its own septic tank in areas of very poor drainage. Incensed by the board's action, and motivated by the obvious need for community planning, Rob and I joined a group of citizens to organize a campaign to incorporate the village. A referendum was held, and Mendota Township was incorporated as the village of Mendota Heights on February 21, 1956. I continued through the next decade to attend Mendota Heights council meetings as more and more stories appeared about development in the village. I was particularly interested in future highway construction, since I had seen the disruption a freeway can cause in an area when I was serving on the Urban League board. In St. Paul, it was people who had suffered; in Mendota Heights, it was the land that was

raped. In the late 1960s, the Minnesota Department of High-
ways proposed building an interchange linking Interstates
494 and 35E and Highway 55 that was to be the largest
intersection west of Chicago. One plan had a section of the
city circled by three freeways and Highway 110, which
would have four lanes. At a council meeting, I referred to this
configuration as the ring of madness. I was not against the
freeways; I simply argued that too much land was being used
to build them.

Using the old political ploy of co-opting your opposition
by appointing them to a decision-making position in government, Mayor Huber asked me to join the newly formed Parks
and Recreation Commission. I accepted immediately, completely aware of his motives and his desire to have me out of
his hair on the highway issue. I became, in fact, Huber's proto-
type of how to put citizens to good use. But I had my own
reasons for leaping at the chance. After attending meetings
about transportation development, I had realized that where
one effected change was not in public discussions of final
plans, but as part of the process that developed the plans.

By 1969, the village had acquired nine undeveloped park
sites, totaling 111 acres. Parks and Rec was to develop a park
system and run a recreational program. The commission
wasted little time, and by February 1970, we had hired a
park planner. That April, on a cold, raw, rainy Saturday, residents planted fifty thousand seedlings that had been obtained
from the Department of Natural Resources. For the 1970–
1971 winter season, I volunteered to oversee the recreational
program. My time was spent ensuring that the ice rinks were
in playing condition for hockey games, scheduling ice time,
and acting as liaison between the hockey program and the
commission.

On August 3, 1971, the council approved the plans for the parks along with a park bond issue of $416,000, and the commission swung into action. I was flattered to be asked to chair the bond campaign, but I declined. Although the women's movement was active in the state, Mendota Heights was a conservative Republican district where the majority of women were homebodies and men were the leaders. Under these circumstances, it seemed obvious that a man would be a more effective chairman. I agreed to arrange the public meetings to sell the bond issue if Jim Schaberg would assume the chairmanship. Members of the commission joined in wholeheartedly as I organized four public hearings in different sections of the village. We won the bond issue vote because of the commission's vigorous campaign and because of support from couples with children interested in a recreational program.

For the next two years I volunteered to run the winter and summer recreational programs with help from other committee members. I loved working with the youth in the summer program, which covered baseball for boys and softball for girls, and in winter, hockey for the boys and figure skating for the girls. When Mayor Huber called me in June 1972 to offer me an appointment to the Mendota Heights Planning Commission, I considered the offer carefully. It would be a wrenching decision to leave the Parks and Recreation Commission. I had found it extremely satisfying to work in my home area, with a group of people who shared the same goals, and to do good work without having to deal with the contentiousness of the civil rights movement, the label of "outsider," and the negative identification with money. Being a member of the planning commission, however, would increase my knowledge of local government. If I eventually ran for public office, my credentials would be strengthened. The function of the planning commission was to ensure the orderly growth of Mendota Heights, in accordance with the city's Comprehensive Plan for Development. I accepted the appointment.

Shortly after I became a member, the commission elected me vice-chairman and, the following year, chairman. Whereas I had refused two years earlier to run the city's park bond campaign, I was now empowered by "women's lib" and embraced the chance to chair a public body. There was no conversation as to how I was to be addressed, even though at the time there was much discussion about the use of the terms *chairman, chairwoman,* and *chair* when applied to women. I never gave any consideration to my title, however, and was perfectly comfortable with being referred to as a chairman.

For five and one-half years I conducted the meetings, finding the proceedings stimulating for the most part and often very challenging. The majority dealt with variances to the city's ordinances, found in the comprehensive plan, and the platting of small pieces of land into subdivisions. The stimulating meetings happened when a developer had a request for a large subdivision. The developer, with one or two members of his staff, and often with a legal adviser, arrived in the chambers ahead of commission members to set up the presentation. The commission demanded a production complete with artist sketches, overlays, and a lengthy oral delivery. These meetings invited lively exchanges between the members and the developer, with his staff interjecting their comments. I controlled the flow of discussion and exercised my prerogative as chairman to cut off the give-and-take when the questions and answers appeared redundant. At public hearings dealing with new developments, citizens had the opportunity to voice their objections. Here again I exercised my prerogative as chairman to judiciously halt testimony, a skill that became fine-tuned.

All developers had their own styles of presentation. One, in particular, was a consummate smooth marketer: he gave the impression that his plat was really better than was required by the ordinances and should be sent on immediately to the council for approval. I enjoyed sparring with him as he tried, in a cavalier manner, to ingratiate himself with me. Another developer I remember was out to overpower us with his delivery. The commission sat on a raised platform, and most people who stood before us were slightly below our eye level. At about six feet, five inches tall, this developer looked us straight in the eye. In May of 1974, he applied with a plan to subdivide a high piece of ground. Each time we reviewed the application, the members of the commission and I expressed concern about drainage and future street development around the acreage. The developer countered aggressively with his arguments, at one point marching out in disgust when I cut off his bullying by saying we would not bend the ordinances just for him.

My time on the planning commission could not have been more productive or rewarding. What greater tutelage could I have had than to chair meetings that ran the gamut from open public hearings to working sessions with the commission and their regular monthly sittings? I felt that I had acquired sufficient knowledge to satisfy the requirements for a master's degree in city planning. All the defining terms used in planning — alley, block, easement, preliminary plat, comprehensive plan, variance, conditional use permit, planned unit development, and many others — were now part of my lexicon. I worked with elected public officials, city administrators, city planners, volunteers who took their responsibilities as appointed public officials seriously, and, finally, with the citizens of Mendota Heights who had sufficient interest in their government to testify at public meetings.

But most of all I relished the dynamism of power connected with the overall good of the planning commission — the orderly development of the city of Mendota Heights. Each time I walked into the chambers, I sensed that here was the seat of local government, and I was an active participant in forming public policy. The chair had the power to manage the proceedings of the commission, and I threw myself wholeheartedly into my job: I liked that feeling of power.

During those satisfying days at city hall, my role as a mother gradually changed. Chou-Chou married Lewis Crampton of Boston on Saturday, November 29, 1969, in our living room. Lewis was divorced, and Mother, a staunch Catholic, was not happy that her only granddaughter — whom she adored — was marrying a divorced man. To solve such religious problems within the family, we decided to have the wedding ceremony and reception in our home. Chou had long since left the Catholic Church; she asked Bill England, a Congregational minister and a Boston University chaplain, to officiate.

To provide sufficient space for the one hundred invited guests, a moving van drove up the morning of the wedding and the movers removed all the furniture from the first floor. We used the first floor and basement playroom to set up tables and chairs for the wedding guests. The buffet supper was served in the kitchen. Chou wore Mother's wedding veil. Her locally made, simple white satin princess-style dress had sleeves of lace and a high-neck lace collar. The lace sleeves came from my wedding dress and the lace collar was put together by Elizabeth Liguori of Kathleen, Inc., from the lace collar of my wedding dress and old pieces of lace from the shop, keeping alive a bit of family history.

Our older children's departures from the family fold were not nearly as wrenching for me as mine had been for Mother. Chou was twenty-five and working as manager of community health for Peter Bent Brigham Hospital in Boston. She had been living in her own apartment in Cambridge for several years and had known Lewis for more than a year. Lewis was a most attractive, intelligent man who had a position with Model Cities in Boston. Almost three years later, on June 3, 1972, Robbie married Janet Horsman in Port Jervis, New York. They had been at Hamilton College together and knew each other well. Because Robbie was a Catholic and Janet an Episcopalian, they were married in an ecumenical service at Grace Episcopal Church.

Our journeys continued in the late 1960s and early 1970s, but Peter and Christopher now accompanied us on our travels, which took us far afield: west to Moscow, east to Bangkok, south to Lima, Machu Picchu, Quito, and Bogotá, and through Mexico. We spent three weeks in Russia in the summer of 1969, because I had wanted to visit a communist country and also to give Peter, who was studying Russian at the Hill School, an opportunity to speak the language. In spite of all the negatives I had heard about travel in Russia, I found it easy to get about. Contrary to rumors, Intourist was most cooperative, and our guides were forthcoming with answers to our questions. Only the guides spoke English, and with the women at Intourist I spoke German to facilitate my requests.

It appeared to me that women ran everything in Russia. They were doctors, lawyers, engineers, street cleaners, farm laborers, teachers, mothers, and wives. There were few women in positions of power in the Communist Party, however. The candy factory that we visited in Kharkov, in the Ukraine, was run by a woman, and all the workers were women.

Our Intourist guides stressed that there was no poverty in Russia. Watching the populace on the streets in the cities, it seemed to me that all shared in a lower-middle-class existence. Nevertheless, the system allowed women access to free education and health and child care, as well as employment and very low cost housing.

Five years later, during a two-week spring vacation in Colombia, Ecuador, and Peru with the boys and Rob, I witnessed how supposedly democratic systems had left the vast majority of their citizens in poverty. Walking through the streets of Bogotá, Quito, and Lima, I was accosted by begging women with children tied on their backs; at the same time, a few elegantly dressed women passed me by. The contrast between the rich and poor was startling. In the early evening, we sat in the plaza where women and children walked together in groups separate from the men. There appeared to be a definite division of the sexes. Because the area was flooded with children, this separation obviously did not extend to the bedroom. I had read about the power of the Catholic Church in South America and envisioned its influence as being dogmatic and structured. But as I watched the women and children casually walk into the church (the men did not appear to be churchgoers), say a quick prayer, talk to friends, and stroll out, I decided that their relationship to the church, so much a part of their daily life, was subconscious. In the United States, most churches are locked during the day for security, and the vast majority of the laity go to church only for Sunday services.

Trips to faraway places where customs very different from American conventions were played out raised questions in my mind. Under communism, Russian women had available all the social services but lived in a totalitarian state. Had they bargained away freedom for security? On the other hand, their lives could be described as better than they would have been under the czars as serfs. In South America's so-called democracies, some women were well off, but the majority lived in poverty. What did freedom mean to poor women who were one step away from starvation and whose lives were dominated by caring for large families? How does one bring about change for women who are disadvantaged when compared with U.S. standards? Do these women want change? I had no answers to my questions, but travel had opened my eyes to women's lifestyles in other cultures, for which I had gained greater respect and understanding.

Upon our return to the Twin Cities Rob was quickly caught up in family discussions that eventually led to the merger of Ridder Publications with the Knight Corporation to form Knight-Ridder. Rob, as were others, was concerned about the presidency of Ridder Publications should anything happen to Bernie Ridder, who was president at the time. No qualified successor seemed apparent, at least to Rob and some others. Rob also was concerned about the number of family members already in or planning to join the business. He felt that outside, non-Ridder partners would be helpful in curbing this practice, which is often prevalent in family-owned businesses. But who was to decide who had what job? And might the women not want jobs? The paramount question, however, was financial: what was the best business deal for the family's financial future?

Discussions had been ongoing with various newspaper chains for a period of time. When serious thought was given to a merger with the Knight chain it was discovered that, because of Federal Communications Commission rules, it could be accomplished only by selling off the radio and television division of which Rob was CEO and president. Rob was in favor of the merger, although it was clear that by voting for it, he would destroy his division and abolish his own job.

Rob and I talked about the dilemma facing him. There was no doubt in my mind that his deep sense of responsibility for the welfare of his sisters would lead him to do what was best for the Victor Ridder family. We figured out that we could manage our investments so that our income would not change substantially; what Rob was forgoing was his salary and the potential increases that came each year. The family urged him to stay in the business, but he replied that he knew little about the newspaper business and had no desire to be part of a large, national public corporation. Rob retired that summer but spent the next two years selling off the broadcast properties, which he had so proudly headed. He and Robbie bought the family radio station in Duluth. My husband never doubted his decision to leave the family enterprises. On the other hand, at the age of fifty-two, I was free from the responsibilities of an executive wife and from the connection to a family business.

CHAPTER 5

I WANT TO BE PAID

Volunteering at the Open School remained a fulfilling experience until the middle of my third year there. It appeared to me that the full-time teachers were no longer including volunteers in activities and planning as they previously had, and that our contributions were less valued. I thought that if I were paid, my standing would be enhanced. An opportunity to test this theory came in early spring of 1974. I read on the bulletin board that the school had received a grant for an urban-rural student exchange program, and that applications to run the program were being received. I applied, emphasizing that I had helped set up the American Field Service Exchange Program in the Twin Cities, had worked with Parents for Integrated Education, and because of my political activities, had connections throughout the state. In an interview with Wayne Jennings, the principal of the Open School, the questions directed to me centered largely on whether or not I understood the time commitment involved. I pointed out my record as a faithful volunteer and stressed that I would devote whatever time was necessary to have a successful program. As the interview continued, I perceived a subtle subtext: "You don't need the money, another person does, and we think you are a perfect volunteer." I did not get the job. The school called in August to ask when I was returning to teach, and only my convent upbringing restrained me from slamming down the receiver. I answered that I had other plans (although I did not).

It is ironic that the first paid educational position for which I applied was funded by the Council on Quality Edu-

cation — the council I had lobbied so hard in 1970 to get
established by the state legislature. When I thought of the
time that I had spent lobbying, the sting of rejection for a job
I deserved throbbed even more. And it compelled me to evaluate further the interactions between professionals and volunteers, paid and nonpaid staff, in different associations. I did
not see the issue as one of sex or race discrimination but a
volunteer's sense of being undervalued. In the decision-making
process, the employee received the final consideration because
his or her job depended on a competent solution, whereas a
volunteer's did not. Even though I had been thwarted in my
first attempt, I believed it was still essential to seek a paying
job to compare the influence I would have against what a
volunteer has. But where?

Late that summer, John Littleford, the new headmaster of
Breck, met with me one afternoon to outline his plans for the
future of the school. He wanted to upgrade the academic program, increase diversity in the student body, and enlarge the
overall enrollment. Littleford was interested in change, in cre-
ating a Breck image that appealed to parents who were
dissatisfied with the public schools and sought a college
preparatory education for their children. To achieve his goals,
the school needed to increase its fund-raising substantially.
He closed our meeting by asking if I would volunteer to start
an office of development at Breck. Stung by my experience at
the open school, I said that if he wanted me, he would have
to pay me. Even though getting a job was on my agenda, I
had not as yet thought about what my qualifications were or
what an equitable salary would be. So I was completely
unprepared when John asked, "How much?" I thought for a
moment and came up with five dollars and fifty cents an
hour. I figured that my time was worth two dollars an hour

more than that of my laundress and cleaning women. He agreed. Within minutes, my status changed from that of a volunteer to a paid part-time worker. I walked out of Little-ford's office overjoyed that my assertiveness had secured me a job — a completely unanticipated event when I arrived for the meeting. At dinner that evening, I told Rob how I had grabbed the opportunity for employment; he supported me wholeheartedly.

I never doubted my ability to run a development office, having managed political organizations and raised funds for political candidates. Like every other woman in my economic and social position, I had solicited for United Way agencies and sold tickets for cultural fund-raisers, not to mention political fund-raising. I joined the staff knowing a great deal about Breck, an Episcopal school founded in 1886. Rob had served on its board of trustees from 1969 until 1973. Even though the school was coeducational, the only woman on the board was the president of the Mothers' Club, and she served ex officio. To rectify the situation, Emily Ann Staples joined the board in the fall of 1972, and I took Rob's place when he resigned in the fall of 1973. After my election to the board, Canon Henderson, who had been the beloved headmaster for more than twenty years, announced he would retire at the close of the 1973–1974 school year. John Littleford had taken his place.

Invigorated by Littleford's plan for Breck's future, I started work in a basement office, assembling names of par-ents to run the annual fund drive for 1974–1975. It was soon apparent that to run a successful campaign, I needed more than an ill-equipped basement room — there wasn't even a phone — and some secretarial help. In addition, I didn't have an official title, making it difficult to accomplish my objective of raising money. By the end of October, after conferring with

Littleford, I was officially listed as director of development with a sunny office in the school administration department and a part-time secretary, George Ann Biros. After research on my part, I received equitable pay when I negotiated a half-time salary based on what a beginning director normally received.

With the most efficient aid of George Ann, and John Littleford's constant checking up on our progress, the annual fund letters were in the mail by the middle of November. John's aggressive oversight did not annoy me. Like John, I was a competitive person who wanted the annual drive to be successful, and working with him was exhilarating. Through my connections with members of Twin Cities foundation boards, I set up appointments for the headmaster to meet with them. Littleford explained his plans for the future of Breck with enthusiasm and intelligence. He outlined succinctly and forcefully that he wanted to transform the school into one with an outstanding academic program using innovative approaches to teaching and with a diversified student body.

At the same time, I saw that the headmaster's aggressive pursuit of change within the school encountered opposition from the faculty, who communicated their dissatisfaction to the former head and parents. Teachers were accustomed to Canon Henderson's more laid-back administrative approach, which gave the faculty a greater say in decision making. The changes happening in the school were not without impact in the development office. The rush of gifts I had anticipated from our annual fund letters did not materialize. Privately, I attributed the lack of response to the turmoil in the school. In addition, some potential contributors were being solicited for both the annual fund and for the canon's retirement fund. The first $50,000 for the latter came from the McKnight

Foundation. (The William McKnights had been prime supporters of the school ever since their grandson, James M.
Binger, had attended in the 1950s.) I confidently assured the
board that the remaining $50,000 would be raised—Canon
Henderson had made so many friends through his many
years' association with Breck. In making that prediction, I
had not adequately factored in that the majority of Breck
parents and alumni were not wealthy. My reputation was sal-
vaged when Elizabeth and John Musser, through whose
generosity the Breck Chapel had been built, gave a matching
gift grant that enabled us to reach our goal of $100,000 by
spring of 1975. At the May 1975 meeting of the board, on
which I still served, I reported that alumni giving had
increased that year and that Breck had raised more money
for 1974–1975 than ever before, combining contributions to
both the annual fund and the canon's retirement fund.

To further both his goals for Breck and my capacity as
director of development, Littleford sent me in February 1975
to my first National Association of Independent Schools conference for directors of development. Here I discovered how
other schools raised funds, and my attendance further confirmed my stature as an administrator within the school. The
administrative position was important to me, for I realized
that I possessed untapped executive skills. The materials presented at the conference reaffirmed the steps I had taken to
start the Breck development office. The various seminars
also corroborated my assumptions that the school was woe-
fully weak in alumni relations and that, in comparison with
most other private schools, the Breck pool of potential givers
had limited financial resources. Breck prided itself on the
makeup of its student body, which was racially and economically diverse. With more confidence, I resolved to concentrate

on alumni giving, a critical component of the school's fund-raising.

But not all was well within the school. The faculty, still riled up by the changes occurring under John's leadership, voted to form a union. The board's executive committee was informed of that action on July 7, 1975, and the certification of the Breck Federation of Teachers took place on September 18, 1975, when the faculty voted twenty-eight to fifteen to form a bargaining unit. Between those dates, the trustees appointed a negotiation committee, of which I was a member. Soon after the faculty's announcement, Dr. Karl Hertz, from the Laboratory School of Chicago, spoke to the board about his school's experience with a union. He strongly advised that the school hire an experienced negotiator and that it be someone with no connections to the board.

Preston Haglin, head of the negotiation committee, was in the construction business and had had a long association with the building trade unions. Using my increased executive confidence at the first meeting of the negotiation committee, I acknowledged Preston's labor experience. Then, echoing Hertz's recommendation, I ventured the idea that it behooved us to engage a lawyer who had expertise in dealing with teachers' unions. Before making this suggestion, however, I had covered several bases. Through telephone conversations with a few committee members, I found support for my idea. And I had had lunch with Peter Popovich, a lawyer who negotiated union contracts for public school boards. Peter and I had served together on the Board of Continuing Legal Education. When the committee agreed that hiring a labor lawyer was a possibility, I recommended Joseph Flynn from the Popovich firm, who agreed to negotiate the Breck teachers' contract.

So began a long and difficult process. This was the first contract to be written between the two parties, and the negotiations dragged on for almost a year. My paramount concern was the question of tenure. A distinguishing characteristic of a private school was its ability to maintain a high-quality faculty, for it had the option of dismissing teachers who did not meet its teaching standards; public school systems, because of tenure, found it almost impossible to fire teachers. I argued strongly that if the negotiating team acquiesced to union demands for tenure, Breck's appeal to parents dissatisfied with the public school system would lessen. The tension over tenure and dismissal, compensation, and the length of the contract became so great that the union threatened to strike at the end of August. It soon became obvious to both sides that a strike was no solution. School opened as planned in September, and the final contract was signed on November 23, 1976, without a tenure clause, and with a satisfactory compensation schedule.

I was relieved when the contract was signed. On an emotional roller coaster during the negotiations, I constantly reminded myself that I represented management. Familiar with Littleford's fast-paced method of operations, I was subtly tugged to be more conciliatory to the union's demands. With time, Joe Flynn taught me that you negotiated each point, you had a bottom-line set of issues you would defend vigorously, you developed a strategy of giving a little here and taking a little there, and, finally, you never forgot that patience was the name of the game. It was a year's course in labor relations.

Listening to the prolonged contract debate over what I categorized as housekeeping details, such as when letters of intent from the headmaster to teachers should be sent, I observed how Littleford's management style in working to restructure Breck's future had negatively affected the teachers' disposition toward him. To put his program in place, there had been a proliferation of faculty meetings; teachers were given additional assignments; faculty involvement with parents at class coffee parties was required; and parent-teacher conferences increased. However, my relations with the faculty were not negatively affected by being on management's side of the negotiating table.

During my second year as director of development, union demands impelled me to evaluate more fully Littleford's style. To begin with, I had thought he made equal demands on male and female staff and faculty, but later I perceived that those demands impinged more on women than on men. In the administrative office it was the female staff who stayed late, finishing paperwork John had generated. He did not seem to consider that they had personal responsibilities at home. The same could be said about the female teachers who went home, attended to their children, and got dinner for their families in time to return for an evening meeting at school.

At one point, John wanted to let my secretary, George Ann, go to cut costs. I asked who was going to replace her. In an offhand manner he mentioned another woman, an administrative secretary in the office, who could do the job. In a horrified voice I pointed out that she was already overworked. My tone must have conveyed how incredible I thought his suggestion was, because he turned immediately and walked away from my desk.

George Ann was not immune from Littleford's requests to do extra work. He had a habit of asking her to stay late to do work just as she was about to leave. I asked that if he wanted George Ann to do work unrelated to the development office to please ask me first. I was in charge of the office and the person to decide about her duties.

Now, within my own sphere of activity, I saw concrete
examples of the duality of women's lives as wage earners and
mothers that I had begun to read about in the monthly publications of women's organizations like NOW. Breck women
endured the demands made on them because they needed the
money. I sympathized with them because, unlike me, who
had financial stability, they could not simply walk away from
their jobs.

These observations, however, did not spur me into
action, nor did the women staff members register any complaints. It was also difficult to accuse Littleford of sexism,
because balancing his covert actions toward women were his
appointments of women to supervisory positions: Kathryn
Harper was named head of the upper school, and Lorraine
Mesken moved from dean of girls to director of guidance. It
was clear that Littleford gave himself so completely to his job
that he assumed everyone working at Breck shared his devo-
tion. He and his wife, Mary, who was lower-school librarian,
lived within a few minutes of the school. They had no children, so they did not experience the family demands made on
other faculty and staff.

By this time my metamorphosis into an active participant in
the feminist movement began to take place. Where I saw an
opportunity to improve the status of women was in Breck's
athletic program for girls. Naturally, after my involvement
with women's organizations and letter writing to Congress,
I was overjoyed with the passage of Title IX in the Education
Amendments Act in 1972 and the enactment of the regulations in July 1975. Title IX bars discrimination in schools
and colleges that receive federal funds. While chair of the
Breck board's long-range planning committee, I remarked
that girls needed more athletics and better facilities. In the

public school systems the opportunities for girls to engage in sports increased immeasurably in the early 1970s. I asked what Breck was going to do. I could not accuse the school of being discriminatory under Title IX because Breck received no federal funds. Instead, I argued that girls' tuition, which was the same as the boys', was subsidizing the boys' athletics program.

John Littleford supported the idea that girls should have equal opportunity. He initiated a series of meetings with Sheltering Arms School, located next to Breck, to lease part of its land as an athletic field for girls' and boys' soccer. In the winter of 1975, Donna Gillman, then director of girls' physical education, described the expanded girls' athletic program at a board meeting. Despite these gestures, those of us who were interested in girls' athletics maintained that much more emphasis was placed on the boys' athletic program than on the girls'.

At a board meeting a year later, Frances Reid and Jean Edblom pointed out that there was a substantial difference in the budget between what was spent on boys' and girls' athletics. Another year later, almost to the day, the board set up a committee consisting of Jean Edblom, Donna Gillman, John Littleford, and me to review the budget for the new school year. The new budget was to reflect a more equitable distribution of funds between the girls' and boys' programs, to better promote girls' sports, and to increase the number of sport teams for girls. We finally got action!

The Spirit of Breck . . . a Journey, a history of Breck School written in 1986, states that "following a suggestion by Kathleen Ridder that girls' tuition partially underwrote boys' athletics, and in response to national equal rights and fitness movements, Breck greatly expanded its athletic program for women." That sentence does not convey the effort and time

it took for Breck girls even slightly to approach parity in
athletics.

Fortunately, the union negotiations did not inhibit
Breck's fund-raising for 1975–1976. The school's annual
fund drive was most successful; we raised $141,000, surpass-
ing our goal of $137,500. One reason for overachieving our
goal was John Musser's matching grant of $5,000 toward
alumni giving. After John agreed to a matching grant during
my telephone request, it struck me how easy it was to raise
money — if you knew where to ask. Under Littleford's tutelage I wrote proposals to various foundations, and the school
received grants of $10,000 from the Northwest Area Founda-
tion, $14,000 from the St. Paul Foundation, and $10,000
from the F. R. Bigelow Foundation. Working with me to
structure foundation proposals revealed John at his best. He
taught me how to write concise declarative sentences in
response to the questions on foundation applications. John
ripped apart my first draft proposal. While he read, he kept
asking, "What are you trying to say here?" I'd tell him. He'd
say, "Then write it." My most successful grant proposal was
for Breck's Concentrated Study Program (BCSP). The idea for
BCSP was an outgrowth of Breck's May study program using
off-campus facilities. In conversations with several directors
of cultural institutions in the Twin Cities, Littleford explored
how their staffs and facilities could be used for concentrated
study in various subjects. When he related these conversations to me, I volunteered to write the proposal, which
entailed designing the program.

I relished my time spent with the institutions' staffs who
wholeheartedly endorsed the program. The proposal stated
that English, mathematics, science, languages, fine arts
(drama, art history, dance), and history would be taught in an

eight-week intensive course covering a year's work. Depending on the course of study, the classes could be held at Breck, the Children's Theatre Company, the Science Museum of Minnesota, the Minnesota Zoo, or the Minneapolis Institute of Arts.

I was jubilant in the spring of 1977, when Breck received $50,000 from the Helen Harrington Trust Fund and $35,000 from the Northwest Area Foundation to support BCSP. I was even more pleased when the headmaster asked me to coordinate the program.

Previously, John had asked me to become full-time director of development in order to manage the capital campaign. For two years, he had been meeting with the long-range planning committee to move us in the direction of a capital campaign. When the board agreed in the spring of 1977 to launch a $2.2 million drive, I was quiet about my skepticism. Instead, I declined Littleford's offer, saying that I did not want to work full-time, but agreed to run the annual fund, along with BCSP, for another year.

Also, I had begun to assess my patchwork of achievements and the challenges that faced Breck in fund-raising. I concluded that a full-time career as a director of development, even in another position, did not excite me. I found that being employed actually inhibited my freedom to express what I thought. The dichotomy between membership on the board of trustees and my position as a school employee, who reported to the headmaster, became untenable. Today, I doubt if a paid employee of a school could be a voting member of its board of directors. Although the question of my dual position never arose while I was at Breck, I gradually developed a sense of conflict between my two roles. As an employee I witnessed the daily running of the school and experienced the various crises. Consequently, I sometimes disagreed with Littleford's positive interpretation of many school events when he discussed them at board meetings. Especially because he was my boss, it was inappropriate for me to dispute his reports.

I began to see new opportunities opening before me. In Minnesota, the women's movement was burgeoning, accelerated by plans for the first national women's conference to be held in Houston that November. As conditions changed, more women were running for political office. Here might be an opportunity for me to pursue elective office. I realized that even though I had only been paid for half time, my commitments to Breck had dominated my life. Adding the Breck experience to my inventory of episodes dealing with sexism made it clear to me that I wanted to be a full participant in the women's movement.

In September, after a family golfing vacation in Scotland, I returned to Breck to organize the annual fund drive and to assist Fred Leighton, the new development director, in taking over the office. Mother went into the hospital in the beginning of October to have tests done because, as she put it, her "plumbing wasn't working right." She died of pancreatic cancer on November 4 at age eighty-two. Her death came quickly, much to her relief and that of my two brothers and me. Mother remained courageous and humorous even at the end. She would not bet with my brothers on the day that she would die because, she said, "I won't collect." I am the one who has collected, the recipient of her sage advice and love that have been a wellspring of support throughout my life.

I was back at Breck in mid-November and worked on the annual fund and coordinated the spring off-campus programs at the Children's Theatre and the Art Institute. I enjoyed immensely my immersion in this innovative approach to education, as I saw what a positive impact the program had on the Breck students. Developing the BCSP proposal and coordinating the program constituted my most creative and exciting time at Breck.

Even though I had refused to be a part of the capital campaign, I was drawn more and more into its planning because the new director of development was not adjusting quickly enough to John's expectations. I ended up in the uncomfortable role of mediator between the two men. After almost four years of modifying my style to fit John's, I was more convinced than ever that it was time to resign. In mid-winter I informed him that I would not return for the next school year because I wanted to run for the state legislature, something I had contemplated doing for a long time. Later, I resigned from the Breck board and completely cut my ties with the school.

These years were important ones, as I had accomplished a transition from volunteer to paid administrator and received a salary increase that acknowledged and rewarded my expertise. What I missed, however, was the freedom of doing what I wanted, when I wanted. I had acquired the wisdom and certainty that, if my newfound goal was to effect change in the status of women, my strength lay in volunteerism. A volunteer chose the cause in which to participate. A successful outcome brought cheers; if defeated, a volunteer could retreat to the home, lick her wounds, regroup, and sally forth with renewed vigor. Because of my past experience, politics was the obvious place for me to further the women's movement.

CHAPTER 6

✎

GETTING TO THE TABLE

lthough I had held memberships in women's organizations, lobbied for passage of legislation pertaining to women, and seen discrimination, I had not yet connected with a community of feminist women. Some younger members were more radical in their feminism than I wanted to be, and the composition of the Republican Party in my county precluded my participation. Having decided to become more active, however, I wanted to talk with other feminists and from these contacts to increase my knowledge of the movement from personal experience.

Within the Minnesota women's political network, I was known as a Republican who gave money to women on both sides of the aisle, if they espoused women's causes. At a DFL fund-raiser for Gloria Griffin, Elin Skinner, whom I had known as a parent at the St. Paul Open School, made a point of urging me to attend the spring 1977 meeting of the Minnesota Women's Political Caucus (MWPC) because there was a scarcity of IR women among the members. I accepted Gloria's compelling invitation, and at that meeting I learned about the conference sponsored by the National Commission on the Observance of the International Women's Year to be held at St. Cloud State University in June.

I arrived at the conference a short while before the pro-family, conservative faction marched out of the convention hall. The Twin Cities papers had been filled with carefully orchestrated pro-life/pro-family accusations that the convention was dominated by radical feminists, lesbians, single

parents, and pro-choicers, who did not represent the women
of Minnesota. Not having sufficient votes to prevail against
the feminist resolutions, and realizing that their slate of delegates to the first national women's convention in November
would be defeated, the pro-family women left the hall en
masse. I was awestruck by the regimental organization of
these women and by their masterful use of the press. The
St. Cloud conference, my first where only women were attendees, affected me like a baptism of fire. Driving home, I was
incensed by the realization that the pro-life/pro-family organizations could defeat the women's movement. Rather than
quietly endure that possibility, I determined to become more
politically active.

My next step was to secure, through the auspices of Ann
O'Loughlin, a GOP Feminist delegate to the national conference in Houston, a ticket for the visitors' section as Minnesota representative Bill Frenzel's official observer. In exchange,
I was obligated to write a summary of the event, along with
personal commentary — an easy task, since I was so delighted
to attend. About two thousand delegates and several thousand visitors and observers attended the meeting, all of whom
seemed to hold differing opinions and very willingly expressed
them. In the visitors' section, I spoke with several black
women, graduates of southern black colleges. They articu-
lated well the problems facing black women who participated
in the women's movement. From our conversations, I surmised that their first priority was the advancement of their
race. The women's movement agenda was dominated by
middle- and upper-class women, some of whom preached
that men were the real enemy. If black women accepted this
tenet, black men accused them of being tools of "whitey."
Black women were thus in a bind: If black males suffered
from both racism and the accusation of oppressing women,

weren't black women playing even more into the hands of the dominant, white population by viewing men as the oppressor? How could black women embrace feminism without fracturing the black community's drive toward racial equality? On the other hand, the black women agreed with white feminists on the need for child care and equitable pay, and shared their desire to have both a family and a career.

During recesses, Chicana, Native American, black, and economically less privileged women complained that many women in the audience and in leadership positions did not understand the situations in which they lived. Compared with them, the majority of us came from affluent backgrounds — in their eyes, I was a rich feminist, an accurate assessment. In my report to Frenzel, I noted the tensions that surfaced at the conference. Despite them, a plan of action was passed that included planks of support for the ERA, reproductive freedom, and lesbian rights. For me the conference was an opportunity to get to know feminists who were younger, radical, and from different ethnic and economic backgrounds. These contacts contributed to my development as a feminist and assisted in my continuing evaluation of where the talents I had accumulated could best be used in the movement.

For the next months I weighed the pros and cons of running for the legislature. Stimulated and encouraged by the GOP Feminists (I was now an active member) and the group's goal of finding Republican candidates for the state legislature who were moderate, pro-choice, and preferably female, I became a candidate for endorsement by the Republicans to run in my legislative district for the Minnesota House of Representatives.

Dorothy Troeltsch and John Pierson, longtime political activists and friends, agreed to cochair my campaign committee. The month before the legislative endorsing convention at

the end of April 1978, I canvassed the delegates elected by
their precinct caucuses, seeking support. There were five
other candidates, all men. My brochure depicted me as a
hardworking Republican who had lived in the district for
thirty years. I wrote that the continued dominance of the
DFL in the legislature and state offices had created an unfavorable business climate, which inevitably endangered jobs,
that the tax structure should be changed to eliminate some of
the state surplus, and that the Department of Transportation
should be pushed to complete the unfinished freeways in the
district. In my short convention speech, I expanded on these
issues and ended with a rousing prediction that an IR candidate would win the district because Republican Gerald Ford
had defeated Jimmy Carter there by one thousand votes in
1976. Each time the delegates applauded, my confidence rose
perceptibly. At the end, I stepped down from the podium,
waving and smiling at the audience, pleased that I had made
such a favorable impression on the delegates. Later, Art
Seaberg, an opponent, told me he had not taken my candidacy seriously until he heard me speak.

After several ballots, it was apparent that as candidates
fell out, the votes were going to Seaberg, a moderate — but
pro-life — Republican, who finally won the endorsement. I
had the satisfaction that my moderate, pro-choice cadre of
supporters stayed with me until I moved that the convention
make Seaberg's nomination unanimous. In Minnesota, pro-
lifers' successes in controlling the Independent Republican
party continued unabated. All three endorsed IR candidates — Rudy Boschwitz and Dave Durenberger for the U.S.
Senate and Al Quie for the governorship — were pro-life.

Work with the GOP Feminists and as a new member of
the MWPC steering committee absorbed me and relieved
some of the disappointment of my defeat. My contribution

checks ran the gamut of organizations — Planned Parent-
hood, Catholics for a Free Choice, NOW, MWPC, WARM
(Women's Art Registry of Minnesota), At the Foot of the
Mountain (women's theater), and the Berg Fund for Women's
Athletics at the University of Minnesota. I envisioned these
groups as pebbles thrown into a pond, which caused such
strong ripples for equity that it would be achieved. The organizations worked on a continuum: the women's political
associations got women and men elected who supported our
positions; they in turn introduced and maneuvered laws
endorsed by the women's movement through Congress and
the state legislatures; then, to ensure enforcement of those
laws, women won court cases that established precedents on
which to base future decisions.

Even with the intense activity of the women's movement,
by the late 1970s I felt that as a new feminist I was treading
water. The backlash had solidified against the ERA, and the
movement was now forced to protect the gains it had made
against the onslaught of the pro-family/pro-life forces. I am
an optimist and a competitor by nature, but the enthusiasm I
brought to my new efforts as a feminist was rapidly ebbing.

After a day of fruitless lobbying at the state legislature, I
dumped my frustration on Rob. In an emotional outburst
about the lack of funds for battered women's centers, I
blurted out, "You know, not all women who are harassed are
from the lower classes. *I* was molested during an interview
for a job at a summer camp!" The episode was a skeleton in
my closet, never mentioned before, which burst forth because
of my anger. Rob was aghast at the disclosure, especially
since the molester was the brother of the headmistress of a
well-known private school in New York City.

I told Rob how it had happened all those years ago.
Mother, desirous that I have a summer job, had arranged an

interview for a junior camp counselor position. When I
arrived for the interview in the one-room apartment, there
was no place to sit but on a daybed. Mother's warning—
"Never sit on a bed if alone in the room with a man"—
flashed through my mind. Yet, I could not stand through the
interview. The conversation began with the man sitting at his
desk. While I explained my qualifications to teach swimming
and tennis, he moved from behind the desk to stand just two
feet in front of me. Suddenly, he was lying heavily on top of
me. I vaguely remember that I stiffened and pulled my knee
into his crotch, and he got up. Standing quickly, I straightened
my dress, ran down the building stairs, and into the subway
station just as a train arrived. Breathless, I took a seat, finally
feeling safe. When I arrived back at the shop, Mother inquired,
as she moved from one customer to another, how the interview had gone. I answered with finality, "Oh, Mother, it was
a useless trip. They want someone who has had camp experience, and I have never been to camp." The last thing I wanted
to do was to tell her what had happened, believing that by
sitting on the bed, I perhaps had precipitated the advance.

The incident, blanked out, lay stored in my memory for
almost forty years. Would I have spoken about it if I had not
been frustrated by lobbying? I cannot say, but the molestation
remained so vivid that its imprint induced me to fight for battered women's shelters when they became an issue. Another
dormant influence on my feminist interests was the barely
audible snatches of conversation I'd hear Mother and Aunt
Kath exchange about how such and such a worker had
arrived late again because her husband had hit her. More
extraordinary is that I never warned my daughter about men
who prey on young women. In looking back, I think that,
like Mother and my aunt, who sheltered me from the crudi-
ties of life, I, too, wanted to shield my daughter.

In addition, running for public office had exposed me to the overwhelming number of advantages white men enjoyed in our society and caused me to think: Would women ever reach parity? Did we have the staying power to achieve success? Women in politics knew that men held the ultimate power, but not until I ran for public office did I see how reluctant men were to share power. Nonetheless, I did not want to be allied with those feminists who railed constantly about the opposite sex, so I refrained from expressing my feelings in public. In my book, not all men were antifeminists. There were certainly men who supported the women's agenda, and I did not want to alienate them with indiscriminate criticism.

Rob supported my commitment to the women's movement. He agreed with me that women have suffered discrimination. Consequently, he resented that he was the focal point of my complaints about men. This harping reached a crescendo in our room at the Ritz-Carlton in Boston, when we were attending Peter's graduation from the Harvard School of Public Affairs in June 1978. Rob said that he had had enough of my antimale tirades. I retorted that I needed him to listen because I had to have somewhere to vent my vexation. After all, I reminded him, I had suffered with him through his alcoholism and supported him until he joined AA. Now I required that same support. He had to understand how thwarted I felt by the lack of women's progress. We traded more words, getting ever further apart. At a high point in the argument, Rob said that the women's movement could not come between us: we loved each other too much. It was a moment of catharsis. Assured that Rob better understood my emotional harangues, I agreed to stop making him the whipping boy.

Over time Rob has counseled me when to detach myself from my emotions and look at events dispassionately. His favorite words are, "Kath, you must remember everyone is entitled to their opinions. Be more logical in your assessment of people. Not everyone sees your grievances as you do. Slow down." When he says this, I do take a deep breath and reevaluate my course of action. Luckily, at these moments of despair, a new avenue of activity can open up for me if I remember to let it.

Like other women in the 1970s I continued to reach the table of political power through the appointment process, but now I entered a new political arena — the judicial system. Justice Robert J. Sheran of the Minnesota Supreme Court appointed me to the state's first Board of Continuing Legal Education (CLE), and I served from 1975 to 1981. The board was made up of twelve lawyers and three public members. There were no female lawyers on the board, and Wenda Moore and I, who served as public members, were the only women.

The CLE board resulted from a study by the Minnesota Bar Association that recommended that each accredited lawyer in the state have forty-five hours of continuing legal education within a three-year period in order to renew his or her license to practice. Minnesota was the first state in the nation to adopt CLE. The discussions, devoted at the early meetings to course accreditation, were most informative, but sometimes seemed endless, as the members jockeyed to get their points across. I saw how forceful lawyers were in advocating their views. In the deliberations, I found my opinion carried little weight at times, but I discovered that the trick was to insert my comments when they were germane to those another member was making.

Drawing on my experience with the formation and passage of laws pertaining to civil rights and women's issues, I urged that courses in this field of legislation be included in the CLE offerings. John Bryon, the chair of the board, told a reporter writing an article about me for *Twin Cities* magazine, "In her non-legal capacity, she effectively presented ideas to the board dealing with problems of the needy, the handicapped, and women that might not have come before us."

The Republican Party won the governorship and the two U.S. Senate seats in 1978. The victory confirmed my position that when Republicans won elections, IR women must be there as advocates for the cause. Eager to further women's opportunities within the appointment process, a group of moderate, pro-choice IR women met to strategize about how our wing of the party could secure jobs for women in Quie's administration. In the middle of December, I was in charge of a meeting held late one cold afternoon at the American Center Building in St. Paul. More than fifty women turned out to hear several women who held positions in the outgoing Perpich administration explain the credentials necessary for specific government appointments and the aggressive lobbying process that they had gone through to achieve success.

Their remarks struck a chord with me. My initial political idealism had been shattered when I assumed, in my innocence, that hard work for a political party resulted in reward. With time I came to know otherwise; my appointment in 1969 to the state Board of Human Rights had been due to the efforts of Kay Harmon, my original political mentor. The art of politics was being in the right place at the right time, but one had to seize the opportunity and work to make it happen. The propitious moment had arrived for me to lobby for appointment to the Metropolitan Council from District 15.

Walter Klaus, my old IR party friend, and G. E. "Jerry" Stelzel, the mayor of Empire Township and head of the Dakota County Township Association, gave me invaluable advice that facilitated my visits with the mayors and chairs of twenty-eight cities and townships in District 15, which included well over the majority in Dakota County. They advised me that the most often voiced complaint against the present council member was lack of contact with the elected officials. In turn, elected officials complained that the Met Council staff were equally inaccessible. At meetings with the elected officials, I focused my pitch on my ability to communicate and promised to be a liaison to the council.

Bob Lockwood, the mayor of Mendota Heights, called after the elected officials met with Governor Quie to say my appointment was guaranteed, because local officials had been so impressed with my interviews that they had enthusiastically recommended my candidacy. Mary Jo Richardson, the governor's special assistant for appointments, called several days later to confirm that the governor had named me for the position. The announcement of the appointment was followed by a twelve-day period allowing for public comment. The governor's office received numerous calls from pro-lifers opposing me, but Quie did not waiver in his support. Mary Jo defended the choice, saying that I was not a single-issue person but a "generalist," an attribute necessary for service on the council. I was jubilant that the pro-lifers were unable to derail my appointment; the Met Council was one of the main public policy agencies in the Twin Cities, and I could not wait to be a member.

The Metropolitan Council was created by the state legislature in 1967 to coordinate the planning and orderly development of the three thousand square miles of the seven-county Twin Cities metropolitan area. There were 273 units of local government within that geographical designation, all with their own elected officials. The council consisted of seventeen seats: the chair and sixteen members appointed for a four-year term from districts of equal population. The chair represented the whole metro area, served at the pleasure of the governor, and was a full-time paid employee. The council members received a fifty-dollar per diem stipend. The work of the council took place in committees with the council board sessions voting on each committee's recommendations.

When I joined the council, its political composition consisted of seven IR members and a majority of ten DFLers. Because of staggered terms and reappointment of members, there was a coterie of well-established friendships. With the exception of Gladys Brooks, whom I had known for years in IR politics, I knew no other members. Despite being a social person who enjoyed people with different political and social views, I felt alone and excluded at my first committee and council meetings. Although I knew that politics played a major role in the appointment process, I was not prepared for the division between the IRs and DFLers on the council. Once appointed, my expectation had been that our political identifications would be laid aside.

If my optimism sometimes misleads me, my pragmatism and ability to perceive reality rescue me. To ensure that my appointments to the various committees from District 15 would receive council approval, I had to lobby votes from the DFL. It was standard political procedure to repay those who had supported one's candidacy by appointing them to committees. There was no opposition to my appointments of Patricia Wirtenan to the Parks and Open Space Commission and Edward Gergen to the Land Use Advisory Committee. I ran into opposition, however, with my nomination of Marvin Edward "Ed" Ramsdell to the Waste Control Commission, because the incumbent DFLer wanted to continue serving. In lobbying for my candidate I had lined up support from all the

IR council members and secured a vote from one DFLer.
Needing one more DFL vote, I called Senator Howard Knutson, who had recommended Ramsdell, for his assistance.
Knutson knew DFL council member Stanley Kegler, the lobby-
ist for the University of Minnesota, who needed the senator's
vote for the university's appropriations bill. Knutson willingly
agreed to assist in getting Kegler's vote. Kegler's vote for my
candidate was unexpected by the DFLers, who thought their
candidate was a shoo-in. Quietly, I enjoyed the victory, confident that my political stature had increased.

Because the population of District 15 had grown rapidly,
and the various governmental entities faced the resultant
problems of such expansion, I was quickly immersed in council work. Part of my job was to shepherd district projects
through the various committees to receive council approval.
An important proposal was the Fairview Hospital Corporation's application to build a hospital in Burnsville, a city in
my district. The Fairview proposal ran into stiff opposition
because it was in conflict with a study done by the Met
Council Health Board and its staff that concluded there were
too many hospital beds and a duplication of services by hos-
pitals in the metropolitan area. In my lobbying, I stressed that
Fairview was not adding beds to the system: it was closing a
hospital in Minneapolis to build one in the suburbs, thereby
maintaining the same number of beds in its system. What
became a contentious issue, and a significant one, was that
the hospital to be closed was in the inner city of Minneapolis.
The media latched onto the issue, reporting on the heated
public testimony of both sides. As a strong advocate for the
Burnsville hospital, I was in the eye of the storm, and the television cameras were focused on me when the vote of the
Human Resources Committee was to be taken. Completely
convinced of the justice of the proposal, I confidently

amended the Health Board's recommendations *not* to build to read *for* the construction of the Fairview hospital. My amendment was easily defeated by the DFLers and Minneapolis City Council members. When the council later balloted, the vote was nine to seven against.

In two years a compromise was reached between the Fairview Hospital Corporation and the Met Council, which permitted the corporation to break ground for the Burnsville hospital in November 1981. Passage was easier through the council because the new appointments in 1981 gave the IRs a solid majority, and Roger Scherer, an IR, became chair of the Human Resources Committee, replacing a DFLer. Also during that time, my ability to negotiate between council staff and Fairview matured to the point where I knew when to ask for compromise from both parties. In a handwritten letter, Bruce Haskins, Fairview's point man, thanked me for all my "vigilant efforts" in supporting their proposal. He wrote that my "persistence and support these past several years had already prompted [Senator] Howard Knutson, a board member, to suggest to us that we name one of the hospital wings after you!" His suggestion was tongue-in-cheek, of course, but to have my efforts so highly praised made me feel good about my effectiveness as a council member.

The most challenging council activity was to conduct public meetings in District 15 regarding development of public policy and regulatory decisions. During my years on the council, the majority of the meetings in District 15 dealt with the siting of dumps for solid waste, garbage, and sludge ash. Terms like sludge, waste abatement, leakage, leeching, resource recovery, storm-water runoff, sewage, scrubbers, and hazardous waste — all dealing with waste management — were suddenly a part of my vocabulary. Their meaning and application became so familiar that I used them with authority at public meetings. The audiences at the meetings could be very hostile: no one wanted a dump in his or her backyard.

With time, resistance to landfills grew ever stronger. The most acrimonious meeting of all was in Farmington, and it was the last that I ran as a council member. "Meeting with Met Council Ends in Shouting Match," blared the headline in the Farmington newspaper in mid-January 1983. The first part of the evening in the high school went as planned, with various officials and residents giving prepared statements. When I asked for comments from the audience, Mayor Patrick Aiken of Farmington, in a loud voice and looking directly at me, proclaimed that it was useless to participate because the Met Council never listened to what was said. In the next twenty minutes, many others chimed in with griev-ances. As accusations filled the hall, followed by applause for each speaker, I realized the meeting was approaching com-plete disorder, and I gaveled for silence. In a controlled, loud, and firm voice, I closed the meeting, saying that the council was following the siting directives of the legislature and that council members seated with me on the stage would be delighted to have individual discussions with audience mem-bers, now that the meeting was ended.

By and large the public was skeptical of the role the council played in fostering orderly development in the seven-county metro area. For this reason, speaking before civic groups or League of Women Voters meetings tested my skills and was a challenge I enjoyed. On the other hand, I steered clear of contact with the media, especially the press, after a public speech. My determination was not ill founded; the public imagined that I had a personal connection to the *St. Paul Pioneer Press/St. Paul Dispatch*. This opinion was shared by state senator Robert J. Schmitz. In a letter to the

My Met Council days

Pioneer Press editorial page he wrote that a February 2, 1983, editorial, critical of the Metropolitan Council redistricting bill, was "unfair, especially coming from a newspaper whose publisher's wife sits as a member of the Metropolitan Council herself," and that it was evidence of a conflict of interest on the paper's part. Below his letter was the editor's explanation that I was the wife of Robert B. Ridder, not Bernard H. Ridder, the publisher.

When my term ended in 1982, I decided to seek reappointment, in spite of being saturated with meetings and weary from driving long distances to run public hearings. I thrived on the constant challenges faced by being a council member. Getting reappointed was a long shot; I was a moderate Republican representing a mostly DFL area. Rudy Perpich, a DFLer, was elected governor in 1982. My only political plus was that I knew Lieutenant Governor Marlene Johnson fairly well, as she and I had started the Minnesota Women's Campaign Fund in late 1982. But that was a thin thread from which to hang my hopes. A political realist, I was not surprised when the list of appointees was announced in May 1983 and my name was not among them.

I was well satisfied with my tenure on the council. All the cities, townships, school boards, and Dakota County sent comprehensive plans to the council by June 1980, the date set by the Land Planning Act. Fairview's new hospital in Burnsville served more than one hundred thousand people in the western part of the county. The uproar caused by farmers against the sludge ash landfills in Dakota County was one of the contributing factors that compelled the council to choose recycling as the way to dispose of the ash. Housing for the elderly was built in West St. Paul, and there was an increase in Section 8 housing for low- and moderate-income families throughout the district. After I surmounted the barrier of being a Republican, I found the staff more than cooperative and willing to answer my innumerable questions, which expanded my knowledge of metropolitan planning enormously.

Leaving was wrenching. I had formed friendships with council members and staff, and for four years had gratified my yearning to be a partner in the formation of public policy. Finally, I would miss the prestige associated with being a council member.

Along with many other women who had received appointments to state boards, commissions, and committees, I was honored at the first MWPC yearly reception in June 1979 at the governor's mansion. The moderate IR women's postelection campaign to seek offices had paid off. To showcase Quie's appointments, I had proposed to the MWPC's steering committee that we celebrate with a fund-raising reception at the governor's mansion. Barbara Forster (DFL) and Marilyn Bryant (IR), cochairs of the caucus, approved the idea along with the board.

A surge of pride—a moment of vindication and reward for my continued participation in the IR party—overwhelmed me when I listened to the Republican governor welcome more than seventy women to the occasion. He praised us for our contributions to the running of the state by serving in our various roles. We were grateful for the recognition, but more important, the reception gave us the opportunity to network and congratulate each other.

An asset I brought to the MWPC board when I joined in late 1977 was knowledge of how to raise money. By and large, women were not big givers to political campaigns. When asked to support women candidates, their average contribution was chicken feed—$5 to $25—in comparison with the $100, $500, and $1000 contributions men gave male politicians. When I solicited, I diplomatically informed the women donors of the obvious: that the cost of running a campaign for a woman was the same as it was for a man. Often they did not get it. Sometimes they answered with a question: "Is the contribution tax deductible?"

To circumvent the tax-deduction barrier, the MWPC established the Minnesota Women's Educational Council (MWEC), a tax-exempt entity to educate candidates and the public about women's issues. Among some of the women forming the council, preliminary discussion of the idea of a fund-raising luncheon brought numerous objections to the $100 attendance/membership fee: Would women pay that much? Wouldn't we be discriminating against those women who were politically active but not able to afford such an amount? It would be viewed as an elitist event. Still others said that they were even tired of going to events where admission was only $5 or $10. I argued that there were women who were financially able to give, and it was up to us to find them. Women would not be elected until women learned to raise money. To prove the point, Marilyn Bryant, Laura Miles (chair of the event), I, and several other women found thirty-two IR and DFL women who gave $100 and signed the invitational letter to the December 5, 1979, luncheon. Women contributed $7,245 to the MWEC that year.

One of the leaders in this new awakening was DFLer Marlene Johnson. In 1981, she and I traveled together on the train to spend Thanksgiving with relatives in Hibbing and Duluth, respectively, and on that trip Marlene enlightened me as to how we could raise "big money" for women candidates. She proposed we ask ten women, five DFL and five IR, to each give $1,000 and form the board of the Minnesota Women's Campaign Fund (MWCF). Marlene reasoned that incumbent politicians had war chests left over from the previous election, and female candidates who wanted to challenge an incumbent found it particularly difficult to raise "up-front" campaign funds. As I looked out the window and watched the snow swirling around while Marlene expanded on her idea, I thought it was as wild as the blizzard raging outside. When she asked me to cochair the fund with her, I declined: where was I to find five IR women who felt so strongly about female candidates they would make a $1,000 contribution?

A month later, after the MWEC raised $13,000 at its annual December luncheon, I sensed that the time had come to go after "big money." I reconsidered Marlene's idea, contacted her, and with my pledge of $1,000 became cochair of the MWCF. It was, and still is, a bipartisan organization that funds progressive women candidates who are pro-choice. It was not nearly as difficult as I had previously thought to find givers. In no time I had convinced five IR women to pledge $1,000 over two years. These women, with the five DFL women, formed the nucleus of the first board.

In early summer of 1982, the size of the board had increased to twenty-five women, each of whom had either given or pledged $1,000 over a two-year period. By the end of 1982 we had $113,832 in income and pledges. The MWCF's phenomenal success can be attributed to the well-known women on the board who, as the first solicitors, developed a list of contributors that was used to persuade progressive women to sign on. Closet feminists around the state took notice of our success and gave. A sense of power emerged as women realized they could be agents of political change. The board granted funds after a candidate had filled out the MWCF's application and research had been done to assure the candidate's pro-choice position and support of women's issues. In the election of 1982, the MWCF funded thirty-one political candidates for a total of $21,200. We would have given more to each candidate but were restricted by election laws.

Along with these MWCF fund-raising efforts, my ever-present aspiration to be elected to the state legislature spun

around in my head. As a result of the 1980 census, Rob and I
now lived in a new district, 39a. We evaluated the possibilities of my getting the nomination and concluded there was a
slim chance. The majority of the delegates to the District 39a
convention elected at precinct caucuses were single-issue pro-
lifers. It crossed my mind that I risked wasting time and
energy on a futile attempt to get the endorsement. Politics,
however, is a fickle business, with highs and lows that are difficult to predict. When I first told some of my old IR friends
of my decision, there were no other candidates running. By
the time I was interviewed by the search committee, two
other candidates had surfaced — one pro-life, the other pro-
choice. Later the male pro-choice candidate, after a visit to
his parish priest, changed his position to pro-life — a switch
that often occurred in the IR party to win endorsement. From
then on, I went through the motions of seeking support from
delegates, knowing it would be an even rockier road to victory. Not surprisingly, the male candidate was endorsed.

The endorsing convention moved me further from the
policies of the IR party. Whereas I had departed from the
1978 IR convention pleased that I had had so much support
from the delegates, four years later these pro-life delegates
expressed open hostility to me as I greeted them upon their
arrival at the convention. Clearly, experience did not matter:
the other two candidates had held no party office. As a
Republican, I had worked hard to do a credible job on the
Metropolitan Council. Governor Quie's office was well aware
of my efforts in recommending IR women for appointed positions in government. Kris Sanda, commissioner of consumer
affairs, and I had instigated a monthly luncheon meeting
beginning in late 1980 of forty IR women who were elected
officials, appointees to positions in government, and effective

leaders in the party. At each gathering, we had either a speaker or a roundtable discussion on a hot political topic. The women in the network encouraged me to run.

But these credentials, plus my years of IR political work, had little influence on the delegates from 39a. In fact, they were a handicap. The delegates resented my connection with the power structure of the moderate wing of the party and association with elected and appointed women. Moreover, many women suspected that I had become a feminist, even though my candidate's speech contained no allusion to work in the general area of human rights, much less feminism.

Ever persistent, I was not deterred by the defeat from continuing to promote women in politics. Having been involved with Rosalie Wahl's 1978 election to the Minnesota Supreme Court, and having formed a close friendship with her, I was anxious to see another woman join the court under Quie's administration. The most logical candidate was Mary Jeanne Coyne, a senior partner in a well-respected Minneapolis firm, whom we knew as a strong supporter of the ERA. Coyne had graduated second in her class at the University of Minnesota Law School in 1957 and was a member of the Order of the Coif, an honorary society of law students, and an officer of the *Minnesota Law Review.* She was at first a reluctant candidate, but a group of women that included me persuaded her to apply. Because of Coyne's excellent qualifications, we were flabbergasted when her name was not among the Judicial Nominating Committee's list of candidates. I had not counted on Coyne's appointment to the Court, but I was irate that neither her name nor the name of *any* other woman had appeared on the list, a strong suggestion that the Quie administration did not consider women eligible candidates.

After James Otis's announcement of his impending resignation from the state supreme court in the spring of 1982, I
called Joe O'Neill, chair of the Judicial Nominating Committee and an old friend of mine from my civil rights days and
the Republican Party. I suggested that Quie name a woman to
the state supreme court, and that the perfect candidate was
Coyne, O'Neill's old classmate from law school. I reminded
Joe that Quie's appointments to the courts were considered
among the governor's finest accomplishments and that to
appoint a well-qualified women would be a fitting climax.
This time my star was in the ascendancy: Mary Jeanne Coyne
was sworn in as a justice of the Minnesota Supreme Court on
September 1, 1982.

By the late 1970s Rob and I joined the ranks of the "empty
nesters." In the fall of 1978 Christopher entered Bates College in New Hampshire after graduation from three years at
the Hill School. Peter had received his M.A. in urban studies
from Harvard. Robbie and Janet were living in Duluth with
their daughter, and Chou and Lewis were in Boston with
their son. Neither of us suffered any trauma from the departure of our offspring: to us it was a normal evolution in our
family history. Each child left with our blessing and encouragement to lead his or her own life. We made every effort to
keep in touch with our children through telephone calls about
once a week. In addition, everyone came home for Thanksgiving, and we vacationed together at least once a year either
in Florida or on Nantucket, believing that the family that
plays together stays together.

The days of my calendars for the years between 1978
and 1982 are filled with one meeting after another. The inter-
play between people's ideas required me to fine-tune my own

The empty nesters in India, 1980

thoughts, especially at meetings where women strategized to further women's social and economic progress. Our successes and failures reminded me of a game of steps, "Captain, May I," that I played as a child. Sometimes the women's movement made giant strides; other times, we had to be satisfied with smaller paces. We were chastened and accused of demanding more than was possible to further equality, forcing us to stay where we were or even to retreat. My commitment to women's equality was at times sorely tested; fairness and justice demanded success. Nevertheless, I was convinced that, slowly and step by step, we were achieving our goal of equality.

In January 1981, at the kickoff reception for the founding of the Women's Consortium, a conglomerate of women's organizations, I was asked to say a few words. I classified myself as a feminist, a Republican, a Roman Catholic, and politically pro-choice. I aroused roars of laughter when I said that it was an identity I found difficult to maintain with Ronald Reagan as president and John Paul as pope. Nevertheless, I did not contemplate changing my colors, but would continue to campaign for women's rights within those established institutions for the next decades.

CHAPTER 7

⁓

WOMEN, THE ECONOMY, AND PUBLIC POLICY

During my four years on the Metropolitan Council, my drive to promote social and economic justice for women did not slacken. In fact, as a member of Senator Dave Durenberger's Women's Task Force, I extended my efforts to the legislative process on the national level. A contributing factor to Durenberger's election in 1978 to fill the remaining four years of Senator Hubert Humphrey's term left vacant by his death was the number of DFL women who had voted for him rather than for Robert Short, the conservative DFLer. To capitalize on this support from DFL women and to sustain it, Durenberger established the nonpartisan Women's Task Force, which I was asked to join. Members from both parties contributed valuable information to the task force's deliberations, for they were well versed in issues confronting women that ranged from the political to the judicial, economic, and social. Our mission was to help Durenberger draft what became the Economic Equity Act (EEA). I envisioned the act promoting equity for women under Republican leadership and shifting the pro-choice agenda to women's economic advancement. I firmly believed that without economic power, women could not achieve equality.

My economic and social status made me very conscious of the power of money. My father had been an analyst at a Wall Street brokerage firm, and early in my life I became aware that money was the fuel that drove the capitalistic system. At the age of seven, I read the weekly stock quotes from the *Wall Street Journal* as my father updated his graphs every

Saturday morning. My mother played the stock market, often getting tips from her customers. On my knees saying my nightly prayers, I fervently stormed heaven with Our Fathers and Hail Marys, imploring that Mother's Campbell Soup, Alcoa Aluminum, and Reynolds Tobacco stocks would go up. If they did, Mother had extra money for my skating lessons, an evening at the theater, or a weekend holiday. Daddy, as a dealer and analyst in bank stocks during the 1920s, prospered until the 1929 crash, when he lost a great deal of money. During the depression, Mother split two-ply tissues and we walked a mile to save a nickel, the cost of a subway ride. I went to both the Brearley School and Smith College on scholarships. My family did not overtly pressure me to get good grades, but I knew the financial assistance depended on academic achievement. At times, I wanted to be like other students whose parents paid the full tuition. Once married with an ensured income, I experienced the relief that comes with considerable wealth. I married into a family that was part of the city power structure, and my understanding of the scope of money's influence expanded considerably.

It took little political acumen to see how men used the power of money to achieve their goals. There were women in my social surroundings who shied away when I spoke about how women lacked personal economic resources and needed to develop them. They considered my belief an infringement on the male prerogative of achieving economic worth and a threat to their husbands' careers. On the other hand, members of the Women's Task Force shared the goal of achieving economic progress, and we were excited that, as volunteers, we were collaborators in structuring legislation to be passed in the U.S. Congress. Our enthusiasm energized us to do the legislative research and connect with Durenberger's Washington office until the EEA was introduced into Congress in

April 1981. By the end of the Ninety-eighth Congress (1983–1984), provisions of the bill covering estate tax reform, day care tax credits, Individual Retirement Accounts, federal farm credit, establishment of day care centers, child support enforcement, and pension equity were passed into law.

My disappointment was that the provision to eliminate discrimination in insurance on the basis of race, color, religion, national origin, or sex was removed from the bill in committee. The task force asked that the actuarial tables based on sex be eliminated and unisex tables substituted. The insurance industry was regulated by the states; consequently, the industry wanted no interference from the federal government. We argued, however, that in the interest of justice and under the Civil Rights Act of 1964, there should be no discrimination in insurance. If unisex tables were used, women would lose some advantages in certain areas, but overall we would gain. In congressional committee hearings, the opponents won because they exaggerated the potential losses for women with statistics supplied by the insurance companies. Although women's organizations disseminated information about the EEA, from my point of view the women who gave so much of their time and effort toward the writing of the act did not receive sufficient public recognition.

The elections of 1982 gave Republicans control of both the White House and the Senate and started a trend to reestablish the traditional roles of women. The members of the Women's Network, formerly the Women's Task Force, which I now chaired, were very conscious of the connection between women, the economy, and public policy. Social critic Barbara Ehrenreich had written that the passage of the ERA was not enough to break us out of our economic ghetto and achieve an equitable wage. We needed an economic approach that was considerably different from anything being proposed in the American discourse of the day. Seeking to redirect the political momentum of the ERA to women's economic status, and to counter the trend toward the traditional woman, I began to see the idea of a national conference as the best strategy. I aspired to bring together a multitude of women's organizations to define the influences that affected women's economic positions. My aspirations might have appeared foolhardy, but I was willing to take the gamble, believing the old adage, Nothing ventured, nothing gained. After all, it wasn't as if there was much ground to lose.

At a breakfast in Washington, D.C., with my old friend Abigail McCarthy, the well-known writer and wife of Senator Gene McCarthy, I outlined my vision for a conference. My enthusiasm caught fire with Abigail. With her political wisdom, built up over her years of knowing the Washington scene, she suggested that we test the idea for a conference with some policy makers in Congress from both parties. I countered that a dinner, paid for by me and hosted by both of us, might be appropriate. Part of my political wisdom was the saying, Whoever pays the piper calls the tune. Abigail suggested further that we consult Susan Hager, of Hager, Sharp and Abramson (HS&A), a Washington public relations firm. Susan was intrigued by the concept of such a conference, but questioned how doable it was. She seconded my idea of a dinner for politicians and other leaders in the movement.

We hosted the dinner on March 1, 1983. Abigail invited Senators Paul Simon and Ben Bradley and Representative Barbara Mikulski to attend for the Democrats. Through my affiliation with the National Women's Republican Task Force and Senator Durenberger's office, I asked Senators Dave Durenberger and Nancy Kassebaum and Representatives

Claudine Schneider and Lynn Martin to attend on behalf of
the Republicans.

The consensus among the group was that even though 63
percent of women worked and 50 percent worked full time,
the workplace was still looked at from a male perspective.
They agreed that policy makers and businesses tended to
think of women's concerns as unrelated to the workforce,
with little impact on the gross national product or the health
of the general economy. Senator Durenberger briefly outlined
what had been accomplished under the EEA. Jill Ker Conway, the president of Smith College, startled the guests with
statistics that compared what American women earned in
relation to men with what European women were paid.
French women earned 86 percent of the average male wage;
Swedish women, 88 percent; Italian women, 80 percent; and
German women, 72 percent. Conway proposed that it was
important to study the policies in those countries that had
been tailored for women. In 1983, American women were
earning between 61 and 62 percent of what American men
earned. The guests gave the idea of a conference high marks,
and the members of Congress pledged their support.

Encouraged by the policy makers' favorable response,
Abigail and I, along with Susan Hager, decided that a conference was a feasible option. Susan's decision to have HS&A
manage the conference was a stroke of luck. Under their
direction, a year of meetings and fund-raising brought the
conference into being. The planning committee consisted of
fifty-nine women representing national women's organizations, unions, women professionals, and national girls'
organizations, with about an even number of Democrats and
Republicans, a political balance called for by the League of
Women Voters. Either Abigail or I ran the meetings through-

out the year in Washington. The extensive network that each
participant had among academic, political, and fund-raising
sources impressed me. We were never at a loss for names of
women to serve as panelists and commentators, and we were
able to tap these same networks when we discussed who
should be moderators for the workshops. Inez Andreas, a
committee member and the wife of Duane Andreas, a well-
known figure in the grain business, gave us our first large
contribution through the Andreas Foundation.

At an early meeting we passed a statement of purpose for
the conference, which read that the committee "believe[s]
there is a need to clarify and highlight the economic role of
women." The conference would "explore women's role in the
workforce, ways to achieve economic equality between men
and women, and ways to focus attention on the value of
women's productivity." A strong coalition of women's organizations supported the conference because the mission
statement echoed parts of their agendas. We titled the event
"Women, the Economy, and Public Policy."

Guided by Ruth Jordan from HS&A, we built a program
around three issues that continually emerged: women as
workers, women and the family, and women and the tax
code. A multimedia presentation, based on papers prepared
by Mary Dublin Keyserling and Julianne Malvaux, would be
developed to give the conference a historical perspective.
Titled "The Status of American Women and American
Women of Color," the presentation demonstrated the role
that women had played in the economic development of our
country through its various eras, concluding with anecdotes
about where women were today and timely statistics.

To showcase congressional support for the conference,
we planned a reception for the twenty-four congressional
women sponsors the evening before the daylong session. Dur-

ing the year, Democratic committee members had enlisted all
the Democratic congresswomen as sponsors; Bobby Kilberg
(a former member of President Gerald Ford's staff and the
Republican Women's Task Force) and I had signed up all the
Republicans. Visiting each of the congresswomen to explain
the purpose of the conference became an intoxicating experience. After each meeting, a sense of political power swept
over me as another member of Congress signed on.

I left those Washington meetings exhilarated by the
progress made in the program's development, but my eupho-
ria was clouded by the uneasy feeling that sufficient funds to
cover expenses were not forthcoming. In addition to the cost
of setting up the conference itself, we would have to pay the
authors of the conference papers and HS&A. We decided on
a registration fee of fifty-five dollars, which was not nearly
enough to cover expenses, and the Women's Equity Action
League agreed to be the nonprofit, tax-exempt agency to
which donations could be sent. Through her contacts with
the American Express Foundation, Ruth Jordan had secured
funds to underwrite the cost of producing the multimedia
presentation. And in the summer of 1983, on a very hot day,
Jill Conway and I presented to the Ford Foundation a proposal that it underwrite the three conference papers. The size
of the Ford Foundation Building and the elaborate furnish-
ings of their offices were quite overwhelming; it appeared to
me that a less ostentatious ambience would have been more
in keeping with their mission of giving money to nonprofits.
After numerous telephone calls and written proposals, they
agreed to fund the papers, but our celebration was limited:
money was still in short supply.

When the tension over the lack of funds approached
panic proportions, I assumed the responsibility of fund-raiser.
(Rob and I had already contributed.) A staff person from

HS&A put together a list of the corporate foundations that supported women's activities. With that list, I started to make cold calls in January 1984. I sketched out the mission of the conference in enthusiastic terms to each potential funder. We ultimately raised $125,000 from thirty-nine donors.

It was a great thrill for me to open the conference of more than 350 women from all over the country with a short welcoming speech. Lynn Cutler, vice-chair of the Democratic National Committee, and Betty Heitman, cochair of the Republican National Committee, also greeted the audience and declared their support for the mission of the conference. Dorothy Ridings, national chair of the League of Women Voters, gave the stirring opening address. The multimedia presentation followed, with the rest of the program running like clockwork.

When Janet Norwood, the commissioner of labor statistics, accepted my invitation to speak at the conference, I felt that her presentation validated the theme of the event. Her speech was so well developed and delivered that otherwise dull statistics came alive. We had to set up more tables in order to accommodate the overflow at the luncheon where Janet spoke, the guests sitting with pencils poised as she related the latest numbers on women in the workforce.

The final panel summarized the workshop proceedings and urged conference attendees to set up similar conferences in their home states. Following the closing, HS&A hosted a dinner for those members of the committee who had played important roles in bringing the conference to fruition. At that dinner, I thanked them for their work and support and ended with a special note of gratitude for HS&A and Ruth Jordan.

My aspirations for the conference had been more than realized: its theme satisfied my craving to advance a cutting-edge issue that faced the women's movement and reflected my innate sense of justice that demanded women's equality in the marketplace. And when one considers that the purpose of the conference was to clarify and highlight the economic status of women in the United States, focusing on policy makers, the committee achieved its goal. We challenged the sixty-four sponsoring national women's organizations represented at the conference to carry the message of the event forward. All of the congressional sponsors or their staff members actually participated. When the conference was over, I felt that, incrementally, progress in achieving women's economic equity would be accomplished. It was a disappointment, however, that the only follow-up conference that took place was in Minnesota. In New Mexico, several women's organizations joined together to study the state's laws and how they dealt with women.

The Minnesota conference, similarly titled "Women, the Economy, and Public Policy: A Creative Challenge," took place in the fall of 1984 and was coordinated by Brooks-Ridder and Associates, Inc. (BR&A), a Chapter S corporation Gladys Brooks and I formed. When Governor Perpich did not reappoint either of us to the Metropolitan Council in the spring of 1983, I approached Gladys with the proposition that we start a consulting firm, a course of action that I had observed other "out-of-work" politicians taking. Gladys was the first woman elected to the Minneapolis City Council and had been the first woman to run for mayor. I was a twice-defeated candidate for public office, but had been appointed to numerous commissions and boards. Because both of us knew our way around the state legislature and had lobbied, we were as well qualified as the next person to consult in areas of public affairs and public policy. Our customers were to be women's organizations, small businesses, and action

groups who wanted political advice. Our services were to
range from polling and research to workshops on politics,
conferences, and a speakers' bureau.

BR&A approached Gloria Griffin, the director of the
Minnesota Women's Consortium, about the feasibility of
having that organization be the sponsor of the follow-up
conference. The consortium board agreed.

The planning committee chose November 15 and 16 for
the conference date, figuring that after the election was an
appropriate time for women legislators and women to network before the opening of the legislature in January 1985.
We patterned the state conference after the national one, but
my role was reversed: no longer a volunteer, I was paid to set
up and manage the conference. Now Gladys and I, in combination with the planning committee, had the responsibility to
draw from the well of qualified Minnesota women to speak
on the conference's various topics.

To provide a national overview for the opening evening
session at Hamline University, we invited Dr. Nancy Barrett,
who had spoken at the Washington conference. Her topic
was "Women as Workers — the National Perspective." She
was followed by a legislative panel of two state senators and
two representatives, equally representing the Democratic and
Republican parties. The women reported on the steps taken
within their parties and the state legislature to foster equity
for women in the marketplace. Each panelist made the point
that more progressive women must be elected to carry forward the women's legislative agenda. Some of the audience
commented later that the speakers were on an ego trip and
politicking. I quite agreed.

The second-day session, held on the St. Paul campus of
the University of Minnesota, began with the multimedia pre-

sentation from the Washington conference. The policy papers
that followed gave an overview of women in Minnesota's
workforce, the role of family, and how the tax code affected
women. The rest of the daylong program consisted of seminars given by panels of women from the media, the legal
profession, social work, and business, which had the largest
number of attendees.

The women's interest in business was also well covered
by Sharon Poindexter, a past president of the National Association of Women Business Owners, who spoke at the
luncheon. The women responded enthusiastically as she
recounted her experiences as a business owner. She urged the
women to be leaders, and if they chose to be followers, to
perform both functions with integrity. Women left the luncheon inspired by her talk.

The conference concluded with Gloria Griffin, who summarized the days' proceedings. She issued a challenge to
implement the message of the conference, wherever possible
and with determination, that women's economic future is
deeply entwined with public policy decisions. To Gladys's and
my delight the comments on the evaluation forms affirmed
that the audience had heard her words. Phrases appeared
such as: "Call the cities of Minneapolis and St. Paul and ask
what they are doing about pay equity"; "More involvement
in legislative action as legislation affects women"; "Distribute
the tax information to my staff"; "Can take ideas, issues,
resources of speakers to organizations I have leadership positions in to disseminate." Mollie Hoben, who later published
the *Minnesota Women's Press,* summed it up well in a letter
to Gloria Griffin: "I am writing to commend you and all the
others who helped plan and carry out ' . . . A Creative Challenge.' It was a marvelous conference! I learned much, felt

touched by the energy and courage of so many women, and
went home with my mind racing. . . . it demanded a lot of
hard work and, more importantly, vision."

BR&A benefited both professionally and financially from
the conference, our first business venture. It was particularly
satisfying that the event was covered in the business sections
of both Twin Cities newspapers, with articles emphasizing
women's participation in Minnesota's economy.

Our next assignment was to work with a group of twelve
women authors who wanted to write a history of women in
business. Researching the files at the Minnesota Historical
Society, I found that there were eleven areas in which women
had worked in Minnesota's past: retail, publishing, manufacturing, milling, trucking, service, restaurants, pharmacy,
tourism and resorts, grocery business, and stationery suppli-
ers. The authors chose well-known women to write about
such as the Borups of Maud Borup Candy, Elizabeth Quinlan
of Young, Quinlan (a Minneapolis clothing store), and Ade-
laide Enright of the milling firm. Discussion about the book,
to be called *Minding Their Own Business,* went along swim-
mingly until we came to the topic of finances. The women all
had work commitments that precluded their taking unpaid
time to write a chapter about a businesswoman. BR&A withdrew from the project after research uncovered no potential
backers.

Meanwhile, BR&A had signed an agreement with the
Independent Bankers of Minnesota (IBM) to be consultants
in staging a conference for women bankers. The IBM was
made up of small banks all over the state. Gladys and I welcomed the chance to work with a planning committee
composed of women directly connected to the financial
world. The conference was titled "Professional Women in

Independent Banking" and covered several issues: an assessment of women in the financial world; an update of the IBM's crucial goals for the 1986 legislative session; an opportunity for women to update their management skills and increase their ability to contribute to the banking industry; and a detailed, up-to-the-minute look into the continuing rural economic crisis in Minnesota.

What pleased Gladys and me most about consulting for this conference was to witness the progress women were making in the economic field of banking. Less than ten years before, a group of women at a bank in Willmar, Minnesota, had gone on strike to protest management's practice of appointing men, trained by the women, to positions over them. The women lost the strike. At this event, the IBM recognized that women were an untapped resource to benefit their industry, and they agreed to spend money to increase their visibility and expertise.

Along with our work with the IBM, we signed a contract with the Minneapolis YWCA. We worked with the Y for three years, primarily as its lobbyists at the state legislature. In the 1986 legislative session, the Y had an interest in eleven different bills that dealt with female-headed families and the feminization of poverty, both issues that came to prominence in the 1980s.

BR&A held a lobby seminar in January 1986 to inform the Y's membership about the legislation and to generate a pool of volunteer lobbyists. Various Minnesota legislators spoke about the social legislation to be introduced into the session. The main attraction was a legislator from Wisconsin who had introduced there an extremely controversial bill that required maternal and paternal grandparents who were financially capable to assume parental responsibility for their grandchildren, if their children could not. The idea was to get young fathers, through their parents, to take some financial responsibility for their actions. A heated discussion followed his presentation without reaching a consensus. To end the meeting, Gladys and I instructed the audience in the techniques of lobbying with an emphasis on the role of volunteers. Informing volunteers how a bill passed through the legislature, how to call their legislators, what to say when they visited with them, and how to interact with animation came easily to us. I enjoyed lobbying, mainly because the process had a specific time frame (the duration of the legislative session) when you knew whether you had won or lost.

During the legislative sessions, under BR&A guidance, Y volunteers and members of the staff testified at hearings for bills dealing with child care, AFDC funding, pay equity, and respite care — all issues that encroached on women's ability to have financial stability and of importance to me. To influence the legislators, a rally was held in the rotunda of the state capitol. Tots from the Y's Child Care Center and children from other centers were wheeled around in strollers by their mothers under the capitol dome. They carried signs to apply pressure on the state legislators.

In addition to our political work, BR&A designed an evening event for the "Women on the Move" committee to promote greater use of the Y's athletic facilities. The committee was made up of young career women, the majority of whom worked in downtown Minneapolis. They were very health conscious; they ran, jogged, swam, and bicycled. Several had the figures of models. They did not smoke; they read books on diet; they ate health foods. The program, called "Brody on Body," featured Jane Brody, the author who writes about issues of personal health. I knew the value of athletics, but health diets — they were out of my league.

By 6 P.M. on the evening of the event, all the exercise
rooms and the pool were filled with men and women. The
buffet, made up of selections from *Jane Brody's Good Food
Book: Living the High-Carbohydrate Way,* was prepared by
Pronto Ristorante. It was such a success that we ran out of
food. As I saw the food disappearing, I sampled a few of the
pasta and rice dishes, but they didn't appeal to me. I related
much more to Brody's talk after the buffet, in which she
spoke about her approach to a balanced life with a healthy
lifestyle.

The Brody evening was a success, but not as challenging
or satisfying to me as our next project with the Y. In a study
done by the association on issues of concern to its membership, equity in education received the most votes. This issue
became the major thrust of the YWCA's Social Action Committee (SAC). I felt keenly about the subject because in the
summer of 1984 I had studied the question of equity in education for girls as a member of a task force established by the
state Commission on the Economic Status of Women. Its
report reaffirmed what many of the committee members
already knew, namely, that because of cultural mores girls
were not encouraged to enter the sciences or math. Information from the Minnesota Department of Education showed,
however, that girls in the fourth grade outperformed boys in
math; they performed at the same level as boys in the eighth
grade, but by the eleventh grade boys jumped ahead. The
task force found that textbooks carried fewer pictures of girls
than boys; anthologies included fewer stories about girls; and
girls' parents did not encourage their daughters to study subjects that prepared them for the new technological age. The
report noted that the most visible change had been in girls'
and women's athletics, primarily because of federal Title IX
regulations. Much to my dismay, no legislation resulted from

the 1984 task force report. The Independent Republicans had won control of the state house, and they pledged that there would be no new mandates with regard to education.

With my intense interest in this subject, I was the BR&A partner who followed the issue of gender equity for the Y's SAC. I scheduled a meeting with Ruth Randall, commissioner of education and a friend of mine, and she suggested that we attend the June 9 state Board of Education meeting at which the board would pass its educational goals for 1988. One of the proposed goals was "to develop and implement a strategy to reduce substantially culture and gender bias in Minnesota school curriculum, instruction, and hiring practices at the start of the 1990–91 school year."

When I saw that gender and culture had been lumped together, my feminism boiled within me. From my perspective, the salient point was equity in education, not cultural diversity. Combining the two issues diminished the importance of educational equity. To alleviate some of my irritation, a staff member of the Department of Education explained that the proposed ruling specified culture and gender because culture was a safer issue. She believed that a combination of the two had a better chance of passing, thus avoiding reaction from the pro-family lobby. After the board accepted the goal, the lengthy rule-making process tested my patience while I attended the state board meetings. There was a constant fear that another objection would surface to hamper the process. Finally, at the December 1988 board meeting, the rule was adopted and became effective June 1, 1990.

Work with BR&A often complemented the activities of my volunteer life. While I was lobbying for legislation at the state capitol, Senator Durenberger's Women's Network continued to gather information on economic issues for inclusion in the Omnibus Economic Equity Act (OEEA), formerly the Economic Equity Act. In the Ninety-eighth Congress (1983–1984) the age of participation and vesting in private pension funds was lowered; the law also allowed women to take time off from their jobs without losing their pension rights. In the next Congress the number of years a person must work to be vested was reduced from ten to five. The single parent in the Tax Reform Law of 1986 (Ninety-ninth Congress) was greatly assisted when the standard deduction for a single head of household was increased and the earned income tax credit expanded. Before this, the single head of household was taxed as a single person who paid more than a married couple with one earner.

At meetings of the Women's Network, we often exchanged political gossip about what was happening at the state legislature. Pat Jensen ignited a meeting in late 1985 with her plan to open memberships for women in golf clubs. She and her husband, Carl, had discovered that their club did not permit women to play on Saturday. They called several other clubs that enforced the same rule. Angered by this discriminatory policy, Jensen proposed legislation to overturn it. She asked what we thought the chances were of getting such legislation passed. We urged her to go for it.

The bill, introduced into the state legislature by Senator Gene Merriam (DFL) and Representative Dave Bishop (IR) and passed in 1986, amended the tax law dealing with the Open Space Act. The amendment read that if a club received a tax deduction because its land was taxed at the rate of open space and not at the market rate, then discrimination on the basis of sex was against the law. Thus, it was illegal for clubs to deny memberships to women or limit women's starting

times. This piece of legislation set the pattern for many similar laws throughout the United States, and the members of
the network applauded Jensen's work.

With each session of Congress the sections of the OEEA
grew longer and longer. The legislation had achieved national
importance in forming public policy that crafted new economic advances for women to achieve economic parity with
men. By the late 1980s, notwithstanding the bill's success,
being a part of the Women's Network no longer engrossed or
excited me as in the early days when the members actually
took part in the shaping of legislation. After Durenberger's
reelection in 1988, meetings were sporadic, and the senator's
office brought no closure to the network, although individual
members continued serving on different task forces such as
child care and Head Start. Chairing his Women's Network,
made up of so many talented women, was a pleasure, and I
am grateful for the opportunity to have helped achieve a
modicum of economic equity for women through the national
legislative process.

On January 13, 1985, I was publicly recognized for my
activities as a volunteer when William Mitchell College of
Law awarded me an honorary degree for my work in the civil
rights and women's movements, and for my role on the
Accreditation Committee of the American Bar Association
(ACABA) in guiding the future of legal education. I was overjoyed to receive the honor and to be acknowledged for my
efforts in those areas. In my short commencement address I
told the graduates what a privilege it had been to work
within the judicial branch of the federal government. I
warned them that there was a public perception that lawyers
were money-grubbers, and I urged them to counteract that
perception by performing pro bono work for the disadvan-

Addressing graduates at William Mitchell College of Law, January 13, 1985

taged. The diversified student body of William Mitchell well understood my admonition.

I served on the accreditation committee for five years. State supreme court justice Rosalie Wahl, the chair of the committee made up of law professors, law school deans, practicing lawyers, and three public members, had asked me to join at the end of my term on the Board of Continuing

Legal Education. Only three women served during my tenure.
I regarded my role as a layperson and public member of the
accreditation committee more from the aspect of a consumer:
will students receive an education that provides them with
the skills to succeed as lawyers? The bar passage rate of the
law schools indicated how well they had prepared their students. The fact sheets that accompanied reports listed the
number of minority students who entered and the number
who graduated. The ABA required each law school to have a
plan that laid out its diversity goals. These plans were moni-
tored: if I noted a low graduation rate, I brought it to the
attention of the members. Likewise, I followed the numbers
of women enrolled in relation to male students. Women graduates increased in numbers, much to my delight.

My comprehension of the legal profession expanded
enormously during my years on the committee, specifically
with regard to legal education. The profession regulated and
evaluated legal education with the ACABA's requirement that
law schools be reaccredited every seven years. The men and
women who served as volunteers on the committee impressed
me with their desire to maintain high standards. The committee set criteria by which each school was evaluated. If a school
was found not to be in compliance, it was asked to rectify the
reasons for noncompliance. This procedure sometimes spread
over a long period of time. When I heard criticism of either
the judicial system or the legal profession, I defended both
vigorously.

I resigned from the ACABA because of a family crisis. On
December 28, 1987, Rob had a heart attack in Moscow,
where he had been with the U.S. Junior Hockey Team. I flew
immediately to Russia. Because the attack had been minor,
we were able to return home in mid-January, but the situa-

tion hit me between the eyes. Could we continue to lead our lives as we always had? Our health had been so excellent that it never inhibited any of our activities. We contemplated selling our home and moving to Washington, D.C., where immediate family lived. Luckily, by summer Rob was feeling well again, and we laid to rest any idea of leaving Minnesota.

I was relieved when BR&A's contract with the YWCA was not renewed in 1989 because the Y was restructuring its organization and pressed for funds. As a result of Rob's heart attack, I wanted to lessen my responsibilities. I retired from BR&A, and Gladys took care of the remaining small contracts before we closed the books in 1990. In assessing our business venture, Gladys and I were content that our work constituted a step forward in the long march toward equity in the marketplace for women. As many other women did at that time, we had fulfilled our desire to have a business of our own. Where we went awry was in running the business on a part-time basis and continuing with our volunteer work. Sometimes an organization asked us to go on lobbying for them, assuming we would do so as volunteers. Once again I perceived a subtext: "You really don't need the money, so why should we pay you?" In actuality, we should have been more aggressive about explaining that we were in business and needed to be paid for our work. If we had been more assertive, our labor would have received the monetary reward it deserved, and, on reflection, we would have advanced the cause of equitable pay for women.

CHAPTER 8

⌒

A Stubborn Catholic

When I introduce myself to anyone as a Catholic, a Republican, and a feminist, a wave of skepticism rolls across the person's face. Invariably, I am asked how I reconcile my feminism with my religion and politics. I stay in the Republican Party to ensure that the feminist agenda remains a party priority, with me, and others like me, present to lobby Republican legislators. Simply put, I am a Christian and remain a Catholic because Catholicism works for me. The church's tradition and liturgy sustain my commitment to Christianity. Since the beginning, change has occurred in the church. My task is now to labor for the institution to realize the centuries-long role women have played in the life of the church, and to permit us, in the name of renewal, the right to imagine and name God from a female perspective.

My knowledge of my religion began with memorizing the Baltimore Catechism. The high point of my young liturgical experience was First Holy Communion. First communicants were treated as a special group of students. We were taken from class for a week to prepare for our first confession and an oral examination of the catechism by the parish priest. We learned some Latin responses and when to sit, kneel, and rise at Mass. By age nine, I had received four of the seven sacraments: Baptism, Penance, Holy Communion, and Confirmation. The girls learned that we could not receive Holy Orders; only men did. We started Bible history in the seventh and eighth grades; the lessons covered some history about the Old Testament prophets and the life of Christ in the New Testa-

My First Holy Communion, 1930

ment, but in eight years of Catholic education I never saw a
Bible. The sisters instructed us that the Catholic religion was
the one, true faith by which to attain salvation. I lived in a
spiritual cocoon, never questioning the sisters' or the catechism's message. My highest grade at St. Lawrence Academy
was in religion. I often received the monthly religion medal
and equally as often the deportment award. Politician that
I was, I always prefaced my requests to sister with "May
I . . ." — the polite way to address a nun and a prerequisite
for the award.

During my grammar school years, I wore two hats: one
as a model student in a Catholic educational environment,
the other in the non-Catholic community of my relatives,
friends in Central Park, dancing school, and athletics. Religious affiliation was not discussed in the family, nor did I
mention religion to my nonschool friends. The one time the
influence of the outside world invaded my school life happened during an interview with the principal of the school,
Sister Chrysostom. Mother had informed the nuns that I was
leaving the academy for Brearley at the end of eighth grade.
Sister warned me that my faith would be challenged because
there were Communists among the Brearley teachers. I paid
no mind to her admonition. I had visited Brearley and was
overawed by the academic program and physical facilities. I
never told Mother about sister's advice because I could hardly
wait to start Brearley.

Sister need not have feared for my faith because, in fact,
my Catholicism became a plus the first year. Mrs. McIntosh,
the headmistress, taught a class in elementary ethics and religion. I was the only Catholic in my section, and the headmistress called on me, whenever it was relevant, to give a
Catholic interpretation of a particular religious point. I discovered that the Baltimore Catechism was useless in discussing

questions that were not solved with black-and-white answers. Mother, who, after leaving Finch College, had taken a course in ethics with Father McSorley, a worldly-wise Paulist theologian, supplied me with the pertinent information I needed. A question that I could not wait to ask her was what was meant by "youth-in-Asia." Mother explained that the word was *euthanasia*. The Catholic Church did not support the concept, saying it was murder: God had an appointed time for each person to leave this earth and be with him in Heaven. In the nonhostile environment of Mrs. McIntosh's class, I became, at the age of fourteen, skilled in presenting a viewpoint that was not necessarily acceptable to others.

History classes exposed the prominent role that the Roman Catholic Church played in the social, political, and economic life of the Middle Ages, a part of the church's history that was new to me. I learned about Martin Luther, Henry VIII, and John Calvin and the effects of the Reformation on the church. The issue of the separation of church and state took on new meaning as I studied the religious wars of the sixteenth century. This newly acquired knowledge about the church did not, however, test my affiliation to Rome.

At Brearley, I was known as a Catholic, but I didn't wear my Catholicism on my sleeve; I rarely talked about religion outside of Mrs. McIntosh's class. I was a quiet Catholic, obeying all the rules of the liturgical year. And I believed in prayer. Mother was a fervent practitioner of prayer; solutions to her life's problems came as "an answer to prayer." Before Christmas of my first year at Brearley, I knew I could not pass my midyear exams without divine help. Mother's most successful means of prayer was the fifty-four-day novena: you said the rosary once each day for twenty-seven days in petition and immediately followed that with twenty-seven days of thanksgiving, even if your petition had not been granted.

I started the novena before Christmas vacation. At the end of the January exam period, all my tests had been handed back with a passing grade, but I had not yet received my French mark. As Madame Champrigand laid my exam on the desk with an F in the upper left corner, I was ready to excoriate heaven. She then picked up my exam booklet to change the F to a D minus. Madame had noticed that the student in front of me with a passing grade had more mistakes than I; she ended up with an F. An answer to prayer had been given before my very eyes.

Because Rob was also a Catholic, no religious conflict arose to disturb my quiet Catholicism. To space our children's births, we agreed to use the rhythm method after our first child was born. Mother gave me the address of the Concip Company in Hobart, Indiana, to which I sent a ten-month schedule of my menstrual cycles. The company plotted the safe periods when intercourse could take place. In discussing the calendar, Mother asked how many children we planned to have. I said six. She answered, "What makes you think that Rob and you are so perfect that you want to reproduce replicas of yourselves?" Her response was unsettling because I had not thought of having a large family as reflective of an overdeveloped ego. Mother's remark made an impression on me, and we decided on four children, rather than six.

Until my first trip to Europe revealed how differently European Catholics reacted to church practices, I thought the etiquette of the American Catholic Church was universal. On Easter Sunday, 1949, in Florence, I wrote in our travel diary: "We went to Mass—advertised to start at 9 o'clock but begun at least twenty minutes late—in Santa Maria Novella. Confusion reigned in the Church with long lines of people waiting to go to Confession, few pews, women without hats, and wanderers everywhere. We went to Holy Communion and returned to find our seats occupied." I was astonished at the lack of formality that prevailed during the liturgy.

The following year we were in Rome for the Holy Year of 1950. We attended the canonization of Jeanne of Valois, the queen of Louis XII and founder in 1501 of a contemplative order of nuns. The Basilica of St. Peter was filled with twenty-five thousand people who had come from all over France. During the service, the French raised their voices in song, singing hymns in French and the Mass responses in Latin. This extraordinary outpouring of spiritual fervor differed from the behavior of American congregations, who rarely, if ever, at that time sang in unison at Mass. Shortly after the canonization, we and three other couples had an audience with Pope Pius XII, arranged through the auspices of family friends. Three cardinals dressed in brilliant red medieval robes swept into the room followed quietly by the pope in a simple white cassock. He spoke briefly to us after Rob identified us as friends of the Hoguet family, with whom the pope had stayed in New York City. I noticed his lovely hands when he blessed us. He appeared ethereal and otherworldly, nothing like his successor, John XXIII, who was large and heavy, the salt of the earth, with a twinkle in his eye.

During the decade of the 1950s the number of American Catholics increased enormously. New parishes were established and old ones expanded. When the pastor of St. Peter's Church in Mendota announced plans to build a parochial school, we left St. Joseph's parish in West St. Paul. In January 1955, the parishioners of St. Peter's gathered at Southview Country Club for a Golden Plate Dinner to kick off the school fund drive. Along with church dignitaries, I spoke at the dinner representing the parishioners. I extolled the advantages of Catholic education, with an emphasis on a child's early spiritual development. In the middle of my speech I thought how much I enjoyed "spinning" this financial appeal for such a worthy cause. The parishioners rallied, and the school opened in the fall of 1957.

At the same time, Father Harvey Egan became pastor. In sermons on liturgy during Lent at St. Joseph's, a priest had spoken about the historical antecedents of the Mass, which helped me understand better the present form of worship. My appreciation of the liturgy increased further under Egan's leadership. Geralda Stanton, the choir director, taught the congregation to sing the Latin Mass responses and encouraged us to celebrate the service in song. The passivity of the congregation was slowly eliminated, and the Mass assumed greater meaning for me.

Intellectually, I was stimulated by the two lectures a year that Rob and I began to attend at the Newman Forum, sponsored by the Newman Center at the University of Minnesota. The forum brought well-known lay Catholics and theologians to speak. While I attended the university working toward my teaching degree (1958–1960), I often lunched at the Newman Center. Whenever possible, I joined the table where a chaplain sat. The conversation was lively and revolved around the new ideas being published by Catholic theologians. Motivated by these discussions, I read books and articles by such authors as Godfrey Diekmann on liturgy, John Courtney Murray on the separation of church and state, Christopher Dawson on church history, Karl Rahner and Hans Küng on theology, and Yves J. M. Congar on ecumenism. Bombarded by the new ideas circulating within the Catholic world, I speculated that if these well-known Catholic academic authorities could question and explore the church's teachings, the door was open for me to do likewise. I abandoned my childlike acceptance of what the nuns had taught me and delved ever further into the new thinking.

More reading prepared me to anticipate that the Second Vatican Council (1962–1965) — more commonly known as Vatican II — would produce sweeping reforms in the church. Because my faith in prayer continued as firm as ever, to make sure that the church opened its window to the outside world, I said the fifty-four-day novena. The Lord answered my prayers. For the laity, the most obvious council reforms were the introduction of the vernacular as the language of liturgy and the fact that the priest now celebrated the Mass facing the congregation rather than with his back to it.

Father Egan embraced the reforms. Not all of the parishioners at St. Peter's welcomed the new liturgy, nor did they applaud the pastor's decision to hire Paul Uselmann, a layman, to be director of the Confraternity of Christian Doctrine (CCD) program. As a CCD teacher, I seconded Egan's action. CCD, the after-school vehicle for instructing Catholic public schoolers in their religion, was the stepchild of Catholic education. Parents whose children attended parochial schools reacted by saying that the pastor no longer emphasized the primacy of Catholic schools in the education of parish youth. I did not share their concern because, with the rise of the suburbs, more and more Catholic students were in public schools. The church was barely building sufficient new churches to keep abreast with this new surge in population, and I thought CCD was a perfectly acceptable way of educating nonparochial school students.

Other parish members criticized Father Egan's activities in the civil rights movement. Egan, a strong advocate for social justice in the church, was a member of the Twin Cities Catholic Interracial Council (CIC). At his urging, I joined the board of CIC. This connection dovetailed well with my membership on the Urban League board, coupling the nonsecular with the secular.

Opposition to Egan's activities mounted after he marched in Selma, Alabama, in early 1965, and it reached such a crescendo that a group of parishioners expressed their complaints to Archbishop Leo Binz. As a result, the archbishop transferred him to St. Therese's parish in the Highland Park neighborhood of St. Paul. His last Mass at St. Peter's closed with the congregation singing "We Shall Overcome." It was a very emotional moment for Father's supporters, especially for me. Harvey Egan, along with the chaplains at the Newman Center, had encouraged me to study, learn about, and understand my religion in greater depth; this pursuit had strengthened my commitment to Catholicism, but my belief in prayer weakened. The rote of daily prayer seemed to be wanting, spiritually unfulfilling. Instead, I talked with the Infinite Being, asking why life was unfair for some and for help in understanding his ways. With Egan's transfer, I witnessed the power of the conservative element in the church who opposed the new order, despite its being sanctioned by Vatican II. I saw, as I had in politics, that it was simpler to issue new regulations than to have them implemented.

Harvey Egan had likewise encouraged my effort to form an ecumenical discussion group, made up of couples from various denominations within the vicinity of St. Peter's. In 1961, Gustave Weigel, S.J., had presented a talk at the Newman Forum titled "The Ecumenical Question: What Are the Chances of the Churches Coming Together?" Since I lived socially and politically in a non-Catholic world, it was natural that Weigel's talk steered me in the direction of the ecumenical movement. I contacted area Lutheran, Presbyterian, Episcopal, Baptist, Methodist, and United Church of

Christ pastors for names of couples who might want to
explore the topic of ecumenism. The Uselmanns and Rob and
I were the Catholic couples. About eight to ten couples met
monthly for more than a year. The glue that held us together
was curiosity about each other's religions. We began our discussions with a comparison of worship and church structure,
moving into marriage, a state in which we all lived. The
stumbling block for non-Catholics was the authoritarian
structure of the Catholic Church, crowned by the doctrine of
papal infallibility. In most Protestant denominations, the
parishes were autonomous, with complete say over their
activities and selection of pastor. Group attendance dwindled
as the discussion about religious similarities and differences
ran its course. The next logical step was a collaborative worship, but the group felt that was too radical and disbanded.

Another of my ideas was to have a diocesan conference
on the Vatican II documents. In a conversation in 1966 with
Father George Garrelts, head chaplain at the Newman Center, I bemoaned the fact that the Catholics to whom I talked
knew little about the documents. With his assistance, I drew
up a proposal; it included a mission statement, the format for
a one-day event, a list of speakers, and a marketing plan. The
audience would consist of leaders from area parishes who
would be trained to return to their parishes to lead mini-
seminars. Patrick Butler, a well-known Catholic in St. Paul,
arranged a meeting with Bishop Gerald O'Keefe and agreed
to support the conference financially. Bishop O'Keefe listened
politely while I told him enthusiastically about what was in
the proposal. I envisioned that as a result of the conference,
Catholics would understand the Vatican documents, and
there might be less opposition to changes. The bishop made
no effort to discuss matters with me and simply thanked me
for my proposal without further comment. As I rose from the

chair and turned to leave his office, I saw him put my proposal in his desk's bottom left drawer—the kiss of death. I never heard a word from him, an indication of how the clergy viewed the laity's input and women's input, in particular.

Parishioners in the pew might not have embraced Vatican II, but for some it was a time of blossoming in the church; intellectual stimulus abounded in participatory programs for the laity. In the mid-1960s, I bought Pierre Teilhard de Chardin's books, *The Phenomenon of Man, The Divine Milieu,* and *The Future of Man.* Pope John XXIII is reported to have said about Teilhard's works, "Do his writings have to be so hard to understand?" Like Pope John, I found reading him a challenge and a test of endurance; it took me more than a year to finish the books. *The Phenomemon of Man,* which I tackled first, had whole sections that I didn't comprehend. The majority of the words themselves were unknown to me. *The Divine Milieu* and *The Future of Man* were easier going. With the help of various commentaries, I understood more and more of what Teilhard said. His exposition of evolution, and the part that we as Christians played in that process, gave meaning and hope to my everyday existence. I was part of an evolutionary process that in time would result in human beings discovering that, at the end of a long creative effort, the Lord and the world will come together in Christ's reincarnation.

At St. Lawrence Academy we had no science courses, so I was left with the impression that science and Catholic teaching were not compatible. From my Brearley science classes, I learned that evolution was a theory of how living things developed from simple to complex. But I was too immature to ruminate about the relationship between evolution and religion. Teilhard connected, and made understandable, the links between science, evolution, and Christian teaching. His use of the words creation, Creator, action, force, progress, attachment/detachment, joy, and love resonated with me. They denoted action, expectation, and hope. I am an optimist, always believing that things will improve, that good will come out of adversity. The espousal of human endeavor as good in and of itself, because it is part of God's creative plan for humans, played into my own feeling that there was joy in activity. Because there is joy, and God created people, we should celebrate that joy.

After I had spent several years as a CCD teacher, Father John V. Flaherty, the new pastor, did not invite me back to the program. His decision grew, no doubt, out of an altercation we had about a new religion curriculum for the high school students. In a meeting in our living room of the high school CCD teachers, Father Flaherty announced that we were to follow the archdiocesan curriculum with no deviations. I commented that, as a person trained to teach at the high school level, I found the curriculum for sophomores to be ridiculously elemental. Father answered that he was the pastor, and I was to do as he said or leave. Rob and I quietly left the parish and went to Sunday Mass with Christopher at the Newman Center, where he made his First Holy Communion.

With the departure came our disassociation from any parish. Unlike some Catholics, whose dissatisfaction with the church prompted them to leave completely, Rob and I remained. Every Sunday, I need the experience of the liturgy. I take the Eucharist as food to alleviate my anger and doubt. The liturgy at Newman, from our very first association, had refreshed me spiritually to such an extent that on Christmas Eve, after the children were in bed, we had placed the presents under the tree, and Rob had kissed me good night, I slipped out of the house to attend midnight Mass at Newman. In the Sunday congregation, besides the students, were worshippers who had left their parishes but worked in the renewal movement. I found a home along with them in the Twin Cities' Association of Catholics for Church Renewal.

The exodus of the laity and clergy from the church in the late 1960s continued unabated. With my unscientific poll, I calculated that one Catholic a week was leaving the church; included in the numbers was our daughter. Although I was saddened by these departures, my allegiance to the church never wavered. Rather than sit back and rail against its awesome power, I stubbornly decided to use my God-given talents to further initiatives within the church. Fortunately, I was asked in the fall of 1971 to be a member of the board of the Ecumenical Institute at St. John's University near St. Cloud. The institute ran a resident scholarship program of one year or six months for ten scholars who did research in the ecumenical movement.

The board met twice yearly at the institute for a daylong session. Often, I spent the night before at the abbey and attended Mass in the famous Marcel Breuer–designed church, enjoying the conversation of the board members and scholars at breakfast. With time, I noticed how few women there were among the scholars. At several board meetings, I spoke about the absence of women; my concern was politely recognized, but never fully addressed.

From the institute's financial reports, it became increasingly obvious that a fund-raising program had to be started. I foresaw a long road of constant cultivation of contributors by the board, a duty I was not willing to assume for an initiative that did not encourage full participation of women in its mission. Also, the romanticism of staying at the monastery and attending Mass faded as the constant visibility of men in black robes at St. John's became oppressive and the physical beauty of the location lost its attraction. I resigned from the board in the spring of 1975. My resignation presaged my transformation in the late 1970s from a passive to an active feminist in the secular world, and the same change took place as I sought social justice for women in the church.

Through formal and informal consciousness-raising sessions taking place among Catholic women, the role of women in the church was being reevaluated. The bishops of Minnesota, cognizant of this awakening, formed a committee to draft a statement titled "Contemporary Woman from the Perspective of Social Justice." More than fifty people — lay members, nuns, and clergy from different parishes throughout the state — took four years and five drafts to compose a statement for the bishops to sign. The result was that in March 1979, the bishops issued two papers — the committee's and theirs — under one title, "Women: Pastoral Reflections."

The paper written by the committee states that women and men are equal, whereas the bishops say equal but with differences that are beyond the biological and that are in accordance with God's plan of creation. In dividing its paper into sections, the committee used headings such as "Woman and the Church," "Woman and the Family," and "Woman and Society." The bishops used the headings "Woman in the Family," "Woman in the Church," and "Woman in Society," not mentioning "Women and Work," as the committee did. To my mind, using the preposition *in* implies that woman's role is subsumed by the church, rather than women being equal partners in defining their role. The true measure of the bishops' concern about the newly emerging woman in the church is contained in this sentence: "We are compelled, however, to mention our distrust of those feminist movements which seem to ignore the God-given differences between men and women, or to equate, indiscriminately, the values of a career with those of a home." Until recently, these

God-given differences between men and women have been defined by male theologians. The bishops cleverly qualified their statement about feminists by using the word *those,* implying that there were credible feminists in the women's movement. The Minnesota bishops deserve praise for issuing both papers in 1979 and further commendation in the late 1990s, in light of the fact that the National Council of Catholic Bishops has yet to issue a paper on women.

Accompanying the issuance of the bishops' papers was Archbishop John R. Roach's Plan of Action. The plan contained a summary of survey material covering women's activities in the church, assembled by a women's task force, as well as a written list of the recommendations made by them. The archbishop concluded the plan with these words: "To make this action plan a reality there must be a system of guidance and monitoring. Within the next two months, I will establish a Commission on the Role of Women in the Church."

Sister Marquita Finley, a member of the task force, informed me that my name had been submitted to the archbishop as a candidate to serve on the Commission on Women. She asked me to accept. When the call came in summer 1979, I listened in disbelief; I was known in church circles for my liberal views. The archbishop ended his request by saying not to give him an immediate answer, but to think about it. He must have read my mind, because I was about to refuse him: I had jumped to the quick conclusion that the commission would be dominated by conservatives and that there was no way I would fit in. After several days' cogitation, however, I decided that it was an opportunity to achieve social justice for women that I must not turn down.

The men and women on the commission were a disparate group: their views of women's role in the church ranged from wanting to protect the status quo to my position of wanting to establish an active commission to bring about change. Building consensus on the commission's purpose took endless time because of the differences of opinion. As one member said, we started every meeting from scratch, not building on the previous discussion. The members finally agreed that to fulfill our mission, we would ask the archbishop to change our status from an advisory group to a full-fledged commission in the archdiocesan structure. We also concluded that we needed an office and professional staffing. By early 1981, the commission had hired Margaret Kvasnick of the Sisters of St. Joseph of Carondelet (CSJ) and opened an office in space provided free in the CSJ Administration Center.

What had greater appeal at the time was my association with a group of fifteen Catholic women who planned to hold a conference called "Women's Quest for Our Future in the Church" at the College of St. Catherine in September 1980. The group, made up of nuns, businesswomen, professors, professionals, and volunteers, joined forces because the bishops' papers and the archbishop's Plan of Action opened a window to design our future in the church. The mission of the conference satisfied my thirst for action as I threw myself into structuring the event. Because of the group's intense dedication to the conference's goal, each member brought her expertise equally and cheerfully to the table, writing papers and designing workshops. My assignment was to locate speakers and manage the day's activities.

At the opening session, I introduced Abigail McCarthy to an audience of more than three hundred women and a sprinkling of men. Workshops focused on six key questions to which Abigail alluded in her speech: How can Catholic women and Catholic organizations affect decision making in the church? Have the stories and myths we grew up with con-

tributed to our difficulties in advancing as women in the
church? What is the significance of public affairs to me as a
Christian woman? How is sexuality, as an expression of the
total person, revelatory of God? Is there a different sphere of
sacred for women? Who are "we" as women of the church,
and what do we envision as our future in the church? The
marvel of the conference was the multitudinous ideas that
sprang from the women in the workshops who were respond-
ing to the clarion call to frame their own future.

The dominant theme that emerged from the summaries
was that the image of women, as developed through the ages,
excluded them as participatory church members and did not
reflect how women saw themselves at that time. A facilitator
wrote that "to the misfortune of both men and women, the
feminine has been culturally diminished as a value of human-
ness. This diminishment is sustained and, indeed, institution-
alized when the Church refuses to admit mature and talented
women to roles commensurate with their potential and experience." Because women feel excluded by the use of male
language in the liturgy, in hymns, and in other forms of
prayer, they called for inclusive language. The conferees asked
for a positive theology of sexuality to counter the negativism
about sexuality within the church. Archbishop Roach closed
the conference with a Mass.

At dinner that evening, he asked me to tell him about the
conference, specifically about the workshop on spirituality
and sexuality. Exuberantly, I summarized the day's events,
which had drawn women from Catholic feminists to mothers
of St. Thomas students who were, on the whole, conservative. After Mass, the archbishop had commented that he was
surprised to see these mothers, which indicated he was also
surprised that all of the attendants were not out of the liberal
mold. Briefly, I outlined the historical points covered by the

workshop: the present-day attitude toward sexuality stemmed from the old Hebrew interpretation of the reproductive process; the Jews, a small chosen tribe, to ensure their numbers, taught that sexual intercourse was for procreation; the Jews believed that the male had the seed (a miniature man) and the female, the soil. Masturbation for men was therefore mass murder, whereas there was no penalty for women's self-pleasuring. Augustine, a man who had engaged in much sexual activity, condemned sexual intercourse other than for procreation when he became a Catholic and priest. I related that the group had addressed one of the workshop's questions: "If God intended intercourse to take place only in relation to procreation, why did he provide such a powerful reinforcer as orgasm to occur at other than fertile periods, and beyond menopause?" The church needed, therefore, to incorporate more fully in its present teaching the idea that intercourse can be an expression of love between spouses, as mentioned in the Vatican II documents.

Looking around the table, I realized that no one wanted to listen any further, especially in the presence of the archbishop! The men were red from their collars to the tops of their heads, and the women's eyes were riveted to their plates. Still, I was glad that I had had the opportunity to relate the proceedings to the archbishop. More than two hundred women had been in that workshop. If the conservative women complained to the chancery about the workshop's positions, at least the archbishop had heard my report first.

Conservative Catholic women did not call the chancery. Nevertheless, they started to dog me. An article about me appeared in the *Minneapolis Star,* in February 1981, stating that I was for legalized abortion. What I had actually said was that abortion was now legal in the United States and, politically, I supported a woman's right to choose. On March

25, 1981, I received a letter from Patricia Wuest, president of the Minneapolis League of Catholic Women, confirming my talk at their annual luncheon on May 18. About two weeks before the meeting, Pat called to say that a group of pro-life Catholic women were to picket the luncheon. I explained my position to Pat: I did not favor abortion; I was for the right of choice. Pat understood my position, and the league stood by me, for which I was most appreciative. At the social hour before lunch in the Hotel de France, women circulated pro-life literature. While handing out leaflets, some of the women pointed me out in the crowd. With equanimity, I continued chatting with the women around me.

My talk, "Choices and Challenges for Women in the '80s," reviewed how women's role in the marketplace had changed, the past political and social influences of this change, and what one could predict for the future. I used numerous statistics and quotes from futurists such as John Naisbett of Yankelovitch, Skelly and White. The talk sounded pedantic as I delivered it, but I had chosen my words carefully, so as not to offend anyone. The speech ended with polite applause. The only fallout came from the actively pro-life women on the commission, who suspected more than ever my advocacy of social justice: to them it really meant I was pro-abortion.

More than three years later, I had cultivated sufficient strength on the commission to initiate an archdiocesan conference titled "Church: Women and Men Relating." A survey we had conducted in the early 1980s recorded that women had made gains in church organizations, but not on parish councils and finance committees, where the power lay. The 1980 conference at St. Catherine's had demonstrated there were many well-qualified women able to be leaders in their parishes. I convinced the commission that the barrier between the church's male culture and women must come down, and that the means to accomplish this was to have a conference that explored how church men and women related to each other.

The fourteen-member conference committee, cochaired by Father Thomas Sieg and me, labored diligently to enlist as cosponsors the Priests Senate, the St. Paul Seminary, the Sisters Council, the Pastoral Council, the Commission on Ministry, and the Archdiocesan Council of Catholic Women. Our most persuasive argument was that the conference followed the archbishop's Plan of Action. The planning committee dedicated more than a year's time to coalescing the diverse ideas, presented by conservatives and liberals, into the conference's goals. Fourteen committees, made up of 140 volunteers, worked on the conference format. On April 3–4, 1984, at the College of St. Catherine, the committee presented a program with two keynote speakers to more than four hundred registrants. The rest of the program took place in seminars devoted to themes: "God-talk: Women and Men Talking with One Another about God" and "Church-talk: Women and Men Talking with One Another about Church Life."

The archbishop opened his talk with a metaphorical statement about my relationship with him, saying that we "live at almost opposite ends of the High Bridge over the Mississippi River and one of these high noons we are going to meet there." He facetiously went on to apologize for his clerical attire: he had looked for a peach-colored jacket at a local tent store, but had found nothing. He thanked the workers for putting together the conference, "a significant step in the advancement of this archdiocese to meet one more of the very difficult, and I think hopeful, kinds of questions that we need to address."

The rest of his speech covered a review of the bishops'
"Women: Pastoral Reflections" and the archdiocesan Plan
of Action. He was forthright in admitting that the pastoral of
five years earlier "does not meet and match the extent of the
wounds and division that separate women from the church in
this our day." In the future, he hoped that men and women
together would find the solutions to issues facing society. I
was encouraged by his remarks until suddenly, right at the end,
he reprimanded us for not having a Eucharistic celebration to
finish the conference because it was a "male celebration." He
expanded on why only a priest could be the celebrant at the
Eucharist. Instead of his speech ending on the positive note
that had pervaded his text, it terminated on a downer. I was
heartsick for the men and women who had worked so hard
on the Celebration of Hope service, in which both men and
women had equal parts. I was particularly exasperated by
these closing remarks because, on March 30, I had conferred
with the archbishop on the entire program. When he asked
about the closing liturgy, I told him that a committee of men
and women from the St. Paul Seminary and the Commission
on Ministry had created the service. The committee thought
it appropriate to have a simple ceremony, where both men
and women said prayers of hope for continuous communica-
tion between the sexes. We had parted cordially.

A multimedia presentation, "Church: Women and Men
Relating," followed the archbishop's talk. I borrowed the idea
of a production from the upcoming Washington conference
"Women, the Economy, and Public Policy." Objections were
raised about the cost, but they vanished when, as finance
chair, I assumed the responsibility of raising the money. The
funds for the conference itself came from the Butler Family,
Elizabeth G. Quinlan, and I. A. O'Shaughnessy foundations
and private support, including Rob and me.

Shortly after the conference, Rosemary Ruffenach, chair of the Women's Commission, received a letter from the archbishop criticizing the multimedia presentation. He wrote that the women and men who spoke of their relationships with the church were too negative; the piece did not portray a sufficient number of people who were satisfied with the church. We thought that a balanced presentation of the pros and cons had been achieved. It was obvious that the conservative element in the church had gained the ear of the archbishop.

Although Archbishop Roach's reprimand and the debate engendered by the presentation hurt, I did not have the luxury of dwelling on my wounds. "Women, the Economy, and Public Policy," the conference that was to take place in Washington that June, diverted my attention. The commission passed a resolution thanking me for the "immense amount of time and energy" that I expended to ensure the success of the conference, and their recognition helped to alleviate some of my disappointment.

The aftermath of the conference forced me to consider whether my membership on the commission was productive in effecting social justice for women. Working with the leadership of the St. Paul Seminary to educate their students about women's issues had led to nothing more than superficial acknowledgment: the seminary curriculum was too overburdened with church issues to address the social concerns a future priest might encounter. The commission had done a thorough survey of the wage scale of women employed by the archdiocese, comparing it with what women in the same positions earned in the secular world. We presented the statistics to the archbishop at our annual meeting in the fall of 1984. Immediately, the chancery came back with its counterattacking figures, justifying their wage scale. The commission let the matter drop. I understood that the archbishop, through control of the commission's purse strings, had complete power over it. Nevertheless, I had hoped that through the church's commitment to social justice, the hierarchy might appreciate women's God-given gifts and reward them equitably. The power of the church hierarchy was not only awesome but relentless. Thwarted once again, and with my approval rating with the archbishop low, I resigned from the commission in June 1985.

My departure from the commission could be construed as a defeat that might have ignited such anger I would have left the church. Although I felt deeply about my resignation, I did not exaggerate its impact; the experience brought pain, but I refused to let it gnaw away at my attachment to Catholicism. In a very short article in *Twin Cities,* published in February 1987, I wrote: "I remain a Catholic because I am stubborn and an optimist. Attendance at Sunday mass recharges me to take up my cross and see if, in the next week, I can bring about a scintilla of change in those centuries of tradition (toward women). My batting average is incredibly low." With the dominance of the conservatives in Rome, I now strike out every time at bat.

Pope John XXIII opened the church's windows to the twentieth century at the Second Vatican Council. I was a laywoman who flew through those windows anxious to spread the gospel of social justice. The windows are now closed; only women who agree wholeheartedly with Rome's teaching on women are welcome. I find that Rome's public preoccupation with women's reproductive rights displays the fear that if women control their bodies, the church loses its authority over them. The church ought to look realistically at the erosion of support for its teachings on sexual ethics, not only

among women but also among men. The men and women of
Western Catholicism support family planning; Catholic
women have as many abortions as non-Catholic.

It is in developing countries that women suffer the most
from the church's constant campaign against contraceptives.
Rob and I have traveled in the countries of western Africa.
We saw women in the marketplaces, seated on straw mats
with children sleeping on their laps, sitting on the ground
beside them, leaning on their shoulders, all barely clothed,
while the mothers sold their meager agricultural products.
The scene made me seethe because the women had no access
to family planning.

I attribute the decline of priestly vocations to the church's
insensitivity to women. In my youth, every Catholic mother
was proud that two or three of her large brood had entered
the priesthood or religious life. There was a brief time when I
thought it was a tradition worth continuing for one of our
three sons. What mother today is going to urge her son or
daughter to go into the service of the church when she feels it
discriminates against her?

The church has alienated women with its images and language, failing to realize that these women were the very
people who saw that their children attended parochial
schools, taught in CCD classes, and worked in parish activities. Ever since the vernacular became the language of the
liturgy, the constant use of the word *man* to denote both
sexes raises a red flag. To the ears of a woman, the word *man*
means a male, not female and male. It has been a constant
theme at conferences, parish meetings, and from the Commission on Women that inclusive language become part of the
church vocabulary. What a blow it was when the Universal
Catechism was published in 1995 to discover that inclusive

language had been left out. One report said that it was the result of politics within the church; if so, the conservatives won again.

Rob and I go to Mass every week, now usually at Assumption Church in downtown St. Paul. The sermons are intellectually more stimulating than the usual fare, with a message that is delivered concisely and without redundancy. I listen carefully for an interpretation that might refer to the role women played in Christ's life. For instance, how easy it would be to point out that when Christ revealed himself to the woman at the well, it was to a woman that he announced the start of his public life. Once or twice a year I am refreshed by the recognition that I am as a woman, not merely as a mother or wife, a part of the life of the church.

On the domed ceiling over the main altar is a fresco of the Assumption of Mary into heaven. At times during Mass the painting prompts a silent dialogue with the church about the images that are used to portray Mary and the female saints. How do I relate to the saccharine rendition of Mary, dressed as a young woman in her blue robes, ascending to heaven with a sextet of angels piping her up? The twelve apostles are on the ground; ten stand looking absently out into space and two kneel, watching Mary ascend. If Mary became the Mother of Christ at fifteen, then the age of marriage, and Christ was in his early thirties when he was crucified, Mary must have been at least in her mid-forties when she ascended into heaven. Women looked weather-beaten and old in the Middle East at that age. Exasperated, I accuse the church of using the fresco as a metaphor of how they want women to exist: docile, virginal, obedient to men's commands, and above all, with our primary duty as wives and mothers.

Reminded at each Sunday Mass how the church views women, my irritation energizes me to work ever harder in the secular world for the equality of women. History has shown that the church eventually is influenced by the social and economic changes that occur in the total community. As women achieve greater equality in the secular world, my hope is that progress will occur within the institution.

My spirit is continually refreshed by my association with people who think as I do, by my family, and by my marriage to Rob. Family exchanges about politics, finances, and personal affairs contribute enormously to my spirit; during our lively discussions we share a lot of affection and respect.

My greatest strength comes from Rob, my partner in marriage. The Baltimore Catechism taught that the sacraments were instituted by God to give grace. How true this has proved to be for Rob and me, joined in the sacrament of marriage. The love, tenderness, and counsel we exchange with each other is a source of grace that regenerates and strengthens us. When apart, we communicate each day by telephone. At home, we discuss, we disagree, we reunite, and we love. My marriage is my wellspring of grace.

CHAPTER 9

~

IT'S MORE THAN A GAME

To fit together the events that paved my path to feminism, the element of chance wound its way in a merry dance — the unexpected telephone call, the random meeting, a political rally, an outburst of anger, the interdependence of my interests with another's, a convention, a meal. At a summer political rally in the late 1970s, I met Vivian Barfield, the first director of women's athletics at the University of Minnesota. This casual meeting introduced me to women's intercollegiate athletics, an interest that has become a consuming passion. In my conversation with Barfield, I congratulated her on how well she had showcased women's athletics and told her of my efforts at Breck. We quickly established that we were kindred spirits in our efforts to promote equality for women, especially in sports. Sometime thereafter, I had breakfast with Barfield and Maxine Nathanson, chair of the Advisory Council for Women's Intercollegiate Athletics at the University of Minnesota. The council, established in 1975 to launch the women's athletic program, acted as a liaison between the community and the department and raised funds for the women's program. With little persuasion, I agreed to become a member of the council. It was a homecoming for me. I was a natural athlete, and sports had played a major role in my life. Women's athletics was on the cutting edge of the struggle for gender equity and was therefore a logical place for me to be. And finally the anger caused by the lack of athletics for the young women of Virginia and stored for thirty-five years found a positive release.

At an early age, I stood a head taller than most of my peers. Mother urged me to capitalize on my height, rather than to see it as a handicap, and engaged me in athletics. I had already started swimming at age five, quite by accident. I'd fallen into the water from our sailing boat off Edgartown, Massachusetts, and began to swim — without a rubber ring! I learned tennis by hitting the ball against the club's backboard. Later, playing tennis with my cousin, Bobby McKenna, who was a year older than I but shorter, I engaged in my first battle of the sexes. He always beat me. Often I ended up in tears, accusing him of cheating. Mother heard my complaints, but quietly told me that I was lucky to have a male cousin with whom to play — little solace for a young girl.

I joined Miss Covington's ballroom dancing school, where at age six I discovered my well-coordinated limbs moved with ease and delight to music. I became one of the star pupils whom Miss Covington called on to demonstrate various dance steps. She thought so highly of my ability that when my parents could no longer afford to pay the tuition after the 1929 crash, she offered me a full scholarship.

By the time I was twelve, my height had already begun to impede my development in the sport of figure skating. Nevertheless, jumps, spins, spirals, and dance steps taught me how to control my body. By the age of fourteen, I wanted to skate the role of "the old woman who lived in the shoe" in the Junior Club's presentation, as part of the New York Figure Skating Club's annual carnival in Madison Square Garden. My hopes were dashed by my pragmatic mother, who explained that all leading parts would go to those skaters who took many lessons, particularly from the pro who choreographed the number. I had taken less than a handful of lessons that year. My disappointment lessened when I was asked to be the line leader for the children who lived in the shoe. I was

chosen because the girl who skated the old woman's part
could not keep time to the music. Ham that I was, I waved to
the applause of the crowd as a long line of skaters weaved
behind me in a series of serpentines and circles. A love of figure skating continued into my adult life, when I became a
national judge.

St. Lawrence Academy provided no sports for its students.
My athleticism matured through endless rounds of "follow the
leader," a jumping-rope game that I played with my friends in
Central Park. When not jumping rope, I roller-skated alone
or with friends for hours on the park's macadam sidewalks.
On hot spring days, I played jacks on the south steps of the
Metropolitan Museum of Art. With my nimble fingers, I won
games of double pigs in the pen and double flying dutchmen.

After Edgartown vacations, the family spent summers
with my grandmother in Rumson, New Jersey. I lived bliss-
fully in this resort world, playing tennis and swimming a mile
a day to train for the club swim meets. I cheerfully played
games with the boys, until late summer of my thirteenth year.
I had defeated a boy in singles who was older than I and who
usually beat me. Excitedly, I told Mother of my victory.
Instead of congratulating me, she said that boys did not like
to be beaten by girls; it was better to give them a good game
and let them win. I was deflated and confused. Among my
peers, I was known as a very good tennis player and swim-
mer. Winning at tennis was more than winning a game: my
identity was centered in my athletic ability. However, like all
girls of my day entering adolescence, I wanted to be liked by
the boys. The rest of that summer, I let them win. Luckily,
that fall I matriculated to a school where my athletic ability
became a prominent part of my life.

I was thrust into Brearley, where highly competitive academic standards prepared a girl for college and where a strong

Seabright Lawn Tennis and Cricket Club in Rumson, New Jersey.
(I am fourteen in this photograph.)

emphasis was placed on sports. My previous eight years at St. Lawrence had not sufficiently prepared me for the ninth grade, so I repeated eighth. Even then, I was overwhelmed by the classwork and fearful of being called on to answer questions in class. It was so dismal that I longed each day for the 2:20 P.M. bell that signaled the end of classes. I would race upstairs to the gym, where my athleticism made up for my poor academic performance. If I had not been good at dodgeball, kickball, beginning basketball, and tennis (I won the

middle school tennis tournament), I'm sure I would have
developed into a basket case.

Academically, light appeared at the end of the tunnel
when I passed all my exams for the eighth grade, several with
Bs. By the tenth grade, I was in the upper third of the class.
Sports had helped me tremendously in my personal development, giving me confidence and the ability to lead.

From the very beginning of my marriage with Rob,
sports were an important bond. We enjoyed participating in
and watching athletic events. Our children learned to swim,
play tennis, and ski, and the boys played hockey. Family
vacations in Florida and Nantucket were filled with many
sets of family doubles and rounds of golf. Since I had stopped
playing golf in the early 1950s, I played tennis once or twice
a week — indoors in the winter — with a group of women.
When Rob stopped coaching boys' hockey in the middle 1970s

*With friends at Sun Valley, just after World War II. (Rob and I are on
the left.)*

and had more free time, we played singles several times a week. Rob is a left-handed tennis player with a wicked cut serve and above-average net game. Naturally, he could beat me. I knew this, but our tennis game irrationally became embroiled in my frustrations connected with the women's movement. To avoid emotional confrontations, we developed a system of rotating serves, each serving eight times and not scoring points. This system worked well until the end of the decade, when I had to give up tennis as a result of a bad ankle — a huge disappointment. Consequently, no one was more pleased than Rob when I joined the Advisory Council for Women's Intercollegiate Athletics. He hoped that council membership might alleviate my chagrin over the abrupt end to my tennis career and be an effective outlet for my ongoing crusade for gender equity.

No sooner had I joined the council than the Department of Women's Athletics was faced with the resignation of its director, Vivian Barfield, in the spring of 1981. Numerous reasons circulated as to why Barfield was leaving. Vivian was an aggressive supporter of women's athletics, which inevitably brought her into conflict with the men's department. Members of her department complained about her administrative ability, saying she spent too much time outside the department cultivating support for women's athletics and not enough tending to the management of the program. I thought that, at least from the public's point of view, Barfield had done a good job. To establish a women's program was a hard row to hoe: you had to lobby for funds from the legislature (the legislature in 1994 provided 52 percent of the operating funds of the department) and share sports facilities with the men, who always had complete access, in order to raise funds from a public that had never supported women's athletics — and do all this with little publicity in the media.

Because Nils Hasselmo, the vice president of administration and planning, asked me to be a member of the search committee for Barfield's successor, I was drawn immediately into the women's athletic program. Of course, I was well acquainted with the importance of Title IX, having been a member of the organizations that lobbied for its passage in 1972. To begin with, women's athletics was organized under the aegis of the Association of Intercollegiate Athletics for Women (AIAW), but there was a movement afoot to have the National Collegiate Athletic Association (NCAA) absorb the women's programs. Acutely aware of the power of the NCAA, I saw the number of women's departments disappearing from the athletic landscape for reasons of financial expediency. The opportunity for women to be in leadership and administrative positions would decrease; plus, the social contacts through fund-raising dinners and conferences for women athletes were bound to dwindle. Without this public exposure, the status of women was diminished, and without status, women lose power. No matter how committed a university might be to equity for women in sports, men were still likely to be athletic directors. Inevitably, more male coaches would be hired to coach women, as a male network developed in women's sports. Under the NCAA, that is what has happened. Today, only the University of Minnesota and five other universities in the country have separate women's departments.

Shortly after Merrily Dean Baker was chosen the new women's athletic director, I became chair of the Women's Advisory Council and a big fan at women's athletic events. When Rob found women's sports just as compelling to watch as men's, he accompanied me. And so began a wife-and-husband collaboration that has continued to promote and finance equal opportunity for women in the sports arena. Often we attended a women's basketball game and a men's hockey event in the same building. Going from one event to another, it was immediately obvious that many more spectators watched the men than the women. Rob and I discussed why the support for women's events was so weak. I blamed the lack of media coverage. He answered that media coverage would come if you had fans in the stands. We were into the "chicken-and-egg" conundrum, which solved nothing. I could do little to get people to attend games; where I saw an opportunity to improve women's status was through fund-raising and my own financial contributions.

Until Title IX, society had considered women outsiders in the athletic world, and men dominated sports. Funds to run the university's men's department came from the revenue sports of football, basketball, and ice hockey and were supplemented by contributions. Among the contributors was a cadre of rich men who gave large sums to their favorite sport.

But how to entice rich *women* to give to a new women's endeavor? By the early 1980s wealthy Minnesota women were giving large sums to other women's causes. In 1983, Mary Lee Dayton gave $1 million to start the Minnesota Women's Fund, a foundation that gives primarily to women's programs. She and Sandra Butler cochaired the campaign that raised another $5 million toward the final goal of $10 million. When asked to contribute to the fund, I declined because I had decided to contribute any large sum to my new interest, women's athletics. Through the years, Rob and I have divided money for donations equally between us, each giving to our own causes. Rob is an unbelievably generous and understanding husband, who backed my financial contributions for women's projects. With our combined interest in women's sports activities, I approached him with an idea to establish a scholarship for a female athlete. "Excellent idea," he replied. Here was an instance in which, because of my financial resources, I could make a real difference. Rob and I established the second scholarship endowment fund for women's athletics in February 1983. (The first had been established by Dorothy Shepard in 1981.) The scholarship is awarded only to students who are upcoming juniors or seniors and have majors in the sciences, mathematics, or the health sciences. We established these qualifications to encourage women to enter these disciplines, in which women have been underrepresented. I have continued to designate a share of my donations to the scholarship, and in 1998 two athletes were recipients. After consultation with Jeanette Link, the director of development, we identified the scholarship with my name rather than give it anonymously. Every year at the Women's Athletic Awards banquet, when I present the scholarships to the recipients, I am grateful to Jeanette for her advice. The pleasure of knowing the awarding-winning student-athletes and watching them participate in their various sports renews my dedication to women's sports.

My knowledge about women's sports greatly expanded when Merrily and I attended "The New Agenda," a national women's sports conference in Washington, D.C., in November 1983. Many sport celebrities, such as tennis player Billie Jean King and golfer Carol Mann, spoke, and well-known women coaches and sports administrators presented papers. The thrust of the conference was the need to open the doors for girls and women to participate equitably in athletics. At that time, an inhibiting factor to progress was the legal case of *Grove City College v. Bell,* which had been filed by the U.S. Department of Education through the Justice Department in February of 1983. In this case, Grove City College, a small institution in Pennsylvania, argued that because it did not accept federal funds, it was not obligated to uphold

Title IX or other federal regulations dealing with gender discrimination. Much to my chagrin, the conference session where the Grove City case was discussed attracted fewer attendees than some of the other sessions. I had anticipated that the room would be overflowing with agitated women who realized the importance of Title IX. From my viewpoint, without the regulations of Title IX, girls and women would not have made the progress in athletics that they had. My political background and work in the women's movement had shown me that without the pressure of Title IX, schools and universities could reduce their support for women's athletics. Grove City won its case on February 28, 1984, when the U.S. Supreme Court ruled that Title IX applied only to programs that directly received federal aid. Those women's athletic programs already in place were not appreciably affected by the ruling, but little progress was made in adding new sports. The forward progress toward parity for women in sports was effectively eroded and was not reactivitated until the passage of the Civil Rights Restoration Act of 1988.

The "New Agenda" conference was my first encounter with a critical mass of women whose primary focus was sports. I had expected to meet other women volunteers like me who were connected with their university programs and were raising money. At the end of much searching I found none. I had looked forward to pooling ideas and forming a network of volunteers — all of us interested in furthering women's athletics. Even though I was disappointed, I returned to Minnesota invigorated by the energy of the conference and ready to work for our women athletes.

My job as chair of the Women's Advisory Council was to enlist council members' aid in fund-raising and be a spokesperson for women's athletics in the community. Fund-raising events revolved around the support of many volunteers under

Jeanette Link's leadership. Some of these people were not necessarily enthusiastic about athletics, but they believed in
giving women the same opportunity to participate in sports
as men. In 1980, we initiated the 100 Women Campaign,
during which women were asked to give one hundred dollars
to support female student-athletes. Mercedes Bates, a vice
president of General Mills and a firm believer in equal opportunity for women, said she would chair the first campaign —
so long as she did not have to attend an athletic event. Mercedes, like well over half of the volunteers and contributors,
was not an alumna of the university.

To expand the role of the advisory council in fund-
raising, I proposed that the goal for the 1983–1984 year be
$100,000, and that each council member be responsible for
$1,000 — either through a personal contribution or by raising
the money. The Berg Fund, named in honor of the well-
known golfer Patty Berg, had raised $87,000 the year before.
Although we did not reach our goal that year, we exceeded
$100,000 the next year.

As professional and volunteer, Jeanette and I made a very
effective team. We attended all money-raising events. It took
no effort on my part to "work the crowd," introducing
myself as chair of the Women's Advisory Council. At the
wine-tasting event, put on by both the men's and women's
athletic departments, many of the pourers were male celebrity
athletes. It gave me particular pleasure to tell them about the
accomplishments of our women athletes, such as our basketball star, Laura Coenan, who was well on her way to being
all-time point scorer for men's and women's basketball, "in
case they didn't know." At the Gopher Golf and Tennis lun-
cheons, I found the crowd most receptive to my fund-raising
message. These women were some of our biggest boosters.

The highlight of my four years as chair of the advisory council was the women's athletic department's celebration of its tenth anniversary on November 20, 1985. Marilyn Bryant was chair. The success of this event can be attributed to Bryant's guidance and her forty-one women volunteers. Early in the planning, she enlisted Don Stolz, the owner, producer, actor, and director of the Old Log Theater, to coordinate the evening's program of twelve celebrity toasters. Stolz graciously donated his services.

Tension developed between the volunteers and some members of the athletic department staff, much to my dismay. During the weeks before the celebration the volunteers energetically solicited sponsors ($1,000) and guarantors ($250), as well as sold tickets; at the same time, they progressed with dinner arrangements, working with the staff. What I saw happening was that certain members of the staff were perfectly willing to give the volunteers the responsibility of selling tickets but they didn't trust them to organize the dinner. The staff often countermanded the volunteer committee's decisions. The situation came to a head over the simple matter of table decorations. A male staff member announced he would do them. Following his announcement there was dead silence and a pall fell over the rest of the meeting. It took numerous telephone calls to quell that fracas and recharge the volunteers. That was my first encounter with the university's lack of sensitivity in dealing with volunteers, a failing that I was to observe repeatedly in the future.

At the dinner, Patty Berg was honored with a plaque in recognition of the fact that the development fund is named for her. In Berg's time at the university there were no intercollegiate sports for women. In 1985, 280 athletes participated in eight sports; the athletes received fifty-six full scholarships

and thirty-eight partial, and the department had a budget
that had risen in ten years from $259,838 to $2.34 million.
The evening program closed with the introduction of the first
inductees into the Women's Athletic Hall of Fame.

While the Women's Advisory Council was devoting all its
energies to the gala, my ties to the university expanded when
I joined the University Foundation board in October 1985. I
was not the first Ridder to be a member of the board. Rob's
cousin, Bernard H. Ridder Jr., publisher of the *St. Paul Pioneer Press* and the *St. Paul Dispatch* and a graduate of
Princeton University, had been president of the foundation
from 1968 to 1973. Rob, who had gone to Harvard, was
asked to join the President's Club, even though the membership was taken out in both our names. The good old boys'
network never thought of me, who actually graduated from
the university, as a potential board member and contributor. I
speculated that they had waited to invite me until I had contributed a sufficiently large sum of money.

At the time I joined the foundation board, the university
was engaged in its largest capital campaign ever; for the next
three years the major part of board meetings was devoted to
reports on that campaign. A total of $365 million was raised,
which included gifts from corporations and wealthy individuals, and those sums were matched with monies from the
Permanent University Fund.

The women's athletic department was part of the campaign, with a goal of $5 million — an unattainable amount,
because the campaign was ill-suited to the potential giving
pool for women's athletics. I divided our pool of givers into
(1) frustrated old-time female jocks who were rich like me;
(2) jocks who had became feminists; (3) feminists who were
not necessarily athletic; (4) men who had been athletes and
had only daughters; and (5) enlightened males who believed

in equality. The historical fund-raising strategy of the department was to start women or men giving annually and then bump their contributions up to $100. Using the campaign as an appeal, the women's athletic department established a chapter of the President's Club, to pull the $100 givers up to $1,000. Contributors pledged $1,000 a year over a ten-year period to the President's Fund, which was usually designated to a specific department of the university.

In the midst of these activities, I was once again on a search committee for a new athletic director. Merrily Dean Baker announced that she was leaving the department in early 1988 to become assistant executive director in charge of women's sports at the NCAA. Chris Voelz, the assistant athletic director of Oregon State, took her place. In her interview, Voelz's well-prepared presentation of her future role in the athletic department came across with an abundance of energy. I valued that energy and her commitment to continue to support the women's department as a freestanding program.

Chris Voelz giving me a "key" to the Sports Pavilion

Since the gutting of Title IX, I had seen the male takeover of
women's athletics happen nationally in both coaching and
administration. Women were losing their leaders in sports,
and I did not want that to happen in Minnesota. Women had
worked too hard to keep their separate departments.

By the end of 1988, the President's Club committee celebrated its goal of twenty members with a dinner of three
hundred guests in Coffman Union, followed by attendance at
the opening game of the NCAA Division I Women's Volleyball Championship. (The number of members has since
grown to about seventy-five, ensuring the department a modicum of financial stability.) I was ecstatic when we arrived in
buses at Williams Arena and saw more than 7,000 fans in the
stands. Part of the agenda for the evening was to showcase
women's athletics for the dinner guests, who were unaware of
the excitement of watching women in sport and the number
of their supporters. The two-day attendance of 17,202 set a
record for the championship. It was a fine accomplishment
for the staff of the department and especially for Chris Voelz,
the new athletic director.

During this period of activity with the women's athletic
department, my intense interest in equal opportunity for
women had me simultaneously embroiled in the university's
affirmative action program. I could not help but observe, at
my first meeting of the foundation board in 1985, that of the
thirty-four members, only four were women. By 1989, after I
had put forth the names of several women as a member of
the nominating committee, seven women's names appeared
on the roster.

Associate Vice President Steve Rozell resigned in the
spring of 1989 as director of the foundation. There were no
names of women or minorities on the final list of potential

replacements, which contravened the university's obligations for hiring as stated in the Rajender Consent Decree of 1980. Marilyn Bryant, Emily Ann Staples, and I took the issue to the Board of Regents. After meetings with the regents and several women of the university administration and staff, our original complaint expanded into a review of how women were faring in the total university community. A staff report was presented to the Board of Regents on April 5, 1990. The report was couched in moderate language, not nearly as strong as I would have liked. Nevertheless, the regents passed a resolution confirming their commitment to affirmative action and diversity.

About a year later, community women attended a meeting to react to the Minnesota Plan II developed by the university's Commission on Women in order to create a more favorable climate for women in the university. I listened with high hopes while Provost Leonard Kuhi spoke forthrightly about the reasons for affirmative action and diversity, saying there was a need for "a change in the culture of the U at all levels." I strongly seconded that need for change: from my perspective, women's athletics was outside the culture of the university. The men's department was not accepted by all of the U's academics, but the department had been around for about one hundred years and faculty members attended their events; we were ten years old, and there were few, if any, at ours.

Energized by Kuhi's words, community women formed a committee we called "Friends of U Women," with Emily Ann Staples as chair, to promote and maintain effective links between university women and community women through collaborative projects and programs of mutual interest and benefit. My personal agenda was to draw links between female professors and staff with the women's athletic program. We met over a two-year period, exploring ways to develop a

large membership pool, which would be offered lectures and
seminars given by women professors. The group did not find
a satisfactory way to form an organization, however, and disbanded. It became crystal clear to me that university women
wanted no outside interference — the university was their territory. In a report, Barbara Stuhler, a committee member and
retired executive associate dean of Continuing Education and
Extension, wrote that community women "viewed University
women as invisible or indifferent to community concerns or
both," and that faculty feared a commitment "beyond their
primary commitment to research and teaching and perhaps
beyond their control."

I was truly disappointed that our committee folded, for it
proved once again that the university did not know how to
use women volunteers. I had chaired a committee of Smith
graduates and professors that raised $2.2 million to establish
an endowment for the Project on Women and Social Change.
I mentioned the Smith project as an example of what could
be accomplished and received no favorable response. Why
couldn't two women's groups get together and function as the
men's network does? I knew that community men and male
professors had many links through grants from corporations,
individuals, and professional associations that develop
through joint projects. As a member of the Advocacy Committee of the University Children's Foundation, I, a woman,
had set up meetings for members of the Department of Pedi-
atrics with government officials, staff, and foundations. It
took no effort on my part, because, like the doctors, I was
committed to advancing children's health.

My disenchantment with one university area was balanced by my simultaneous success as cochair of fund-raising
for the new athletic facilities. With greater clarity of vision, I

might have realized before I immersed myself in affirmative action that to focus on athletics was a better expenditure of energy. (Moreover, Chris Voelz *encouraged* volunteers to be an integral part of the program.) The facilities at the university for men's basketball and hockey were commonly referred to as "antiquated." The women's basketball, gymnastics, and volleyball teams used Williams Arena, the men's basketball home. In June 1990, the Board of Regents approved preliminary plans that included a new hockey rink, renovation of Williams Arena for men's basketball, and the revamping of Mariucci Ice Arena into a sports pavilion, to be used primarily by the women's department. Chris Voelz had kept me abreast of the plans, so I was not completely surprised when she asked me to cochair, with Stan Hubbard, owner of KSTP radio and television, the fund-raising campaign. The most persuasive argument for accepting the job was that women athletes would gain a venue with which the public would identify them. I envisioned a building with a large "Ms." (the women's department logo) over the front entrance.

That image was destroyed in the planning process by the men's department's oh-so-magnanimous proposal that Bierman, a small athletic area attached to the administration building, be renovated to provide a facility with a seating capacity of about two thousand for women's athletics. I was livid and let it be known that I would have nothing to do with a "high school facility" for university women's athletics. The advisory council agreed with me, and at a meeting on March 12, 1991, the council unanimously endorsed the original plans approved by the Board of Regents.

A key player on our side was Bob Erickson, vice president for university finance. In a conversation with him during the crisis, I had emphasized how important it was for the uni-

versity to be visible in its support of equality for women by
building the Sports Pavilion; he understood completely and
became our advocate, for which I will be ever thankful.
Finally, as a result of the council's advocacy and a bit of inter-
nal homework on the part of the university, the original plan
was back on track. Inwardly, I was jubilant: for once we had
won. Outwardly, I kept my cool; I had learned to keep my
passion for equality for women athletes under control, for to
appear too strident accomplished little.

After the Board of Regents accepted the facilities plan at
their June 1991 meeting, fund-raising began in earnest.
Assisting Stan Hubbard and me were well-known former
men athletes "Pinky" McNamara, Billy Bye, Bruce Telander,
John Mayasich, and Charles "Chuck" Mencel, who were in
charge of major gifts. An executive committee consisting of
volunteers from both the women's and men's advisory councils, the chairs of the gift committees, and the development
staff met monthly throughout most of the campaign. More
than thirty-five dedicated volunteers, the vast majority of
whom were men, solicited funds. Keeping tabs most effectively on the committee chairs and volunteers was Jan
Unstad, the development officer for the campaign. I enjoyed
working with Jan; she was another woman in a sea of men.

What was it like being the only active female volunteer in
the campaign? It was not the first time I was the lone woman
on a committee. I had developed the practice of reading the
sports pages of the newspaper thoroughly before I attended
such meetings: sports was the common language of men. I
ran most of the meetings because Stan Hubbard had alerted
us that his schedule would often take him out of town. I
knew the members of the hockey committee through Rob's
association with the Gopher teams. I did not know the bas-

ketball committee, and affiliation with the men's department
was a tenuous one. As often happens when there is limited
contact with a department, there were situations when I felt
left out of the loop. I did not mention these incidents, for I
wanted to maintain cordial relations until the funds were
raised and the facilities — particularly the Sports Pavilion —
were built.

The dedication of the Sports Pavilion took place on
December 12, 1993, and held great poignancy and drama for
me. Women's athletics had a home of its own! And there
blazed a lighted "Ms." emblem over its entrance. Governor
Arne Carlson opened the ceremonies and called it a great day
for women athletes to have such a first-class facility in which
to play. My remarks stressed that the pavilion was a fitting
climax to the growth of women's athletics over the past
twenty years. I looked around at the three thousand spectators and expressed my heartfelt thanks to them for their
support that had made the pavilion possible.

The icing on the cake, and the biggest reward for all
my efforts, was another ceremony at the Sports Pavilion in
January 1994. Contributors who gave a specific amount of
money were eligible for various naming opportunities. My
contribution, along with Rob's, gave us such an opportunity, and we chose to call the entrance to the pavilion the
Kathleen C. Ridder Lobby. Between periods of the Min-
nesota-Iowa basketball game, President Hasselmo, Chris
Voelz, and I walked out to the center of the court for what I
thought was to be a purely perfunctory presentation of the
plaque that would hang in the lobby. After Hasselmo presented me with the naming plaque, Chris congratulated me,
and I looked up to see a standing ovation! Stunned, I was
nearly overcome by the gracious recognition they awarded

The presentation of the plaque for the Kathleen C. Ridder Lobby at the Sports Pavilion, January 1994

me. In the quiet behind the stands Rob and I embraced, and I thanked him for his unstinting support. "Oh, Tootsie," he answered, "what fun it has been!"

The women's athletic department celebrated its twentieth anniversary in 1995; for the same number of years, I had been actively associated with women in sports. What progress has been made? Women's soccer was added at the university in 1993 because so many young girls were playing the game in Minnesota. A committee made up of women and men ice hockey enthusiasts, including my husband, staged the first national women's ice hockey championships at Mariucci Arena in the fall of 1993. Twelve high schools had ice hockey for girls during the winter of 1994–1995, and throughout the nation the increase in the number of girls and women participating in sports is remarkable.

Where we have fallen behind is in the administration of our sports and the lack of female coaches. In 1972, studies showed that 90 percent of women's programs in high schools, colleges, and universities were administered by women. By 1990, 84.1 percent of women's programs were headed by men in combined departments. The picture in coaching is the same: almost all women were coached by women in the early 1970s; by the 1990s, 53 percent of the coaches were men. The most discouraging statistic of all is the decline in the number of separate athletic programs for women: in 1985, there were ten such departments; in 1995, there were six. It is more imperative than ever that we continue to ensure that the University of Minnesota maintains its separate programs for women and men.

Coverage in the sports pages of girls' and women's activities is slowly improving. Some of the local male columnists are still very negative, and as recently as 1994, one described several of the more active volunteers, including me, as "those rich downtown women." It still upsets me that wealthy men can support male athletes and not be referred to derogatorily, but their female counterparts are criticized. Rather than be angered by the snide remark, I have turned the appellation around to mean that we rich women finally understand that the name of the game is money. My goal is to continue raising money for scholarships and facilities so that women will be guaranteed a level athletic playing field with men. To achieve that end, women must be constantly vigilant in order to frustrate any activity on the part of the male sports world to sabotage our successes and to weaken Title IX regulations.

The inspiration that fuels my passion is the student-athletes at the University of Minnesota. The women's athletic department has the highest grade point average of any university unit. These young women graduate not only with high academic marks but also with valuable skills that they have acquired through their participation in sports. In competition, they learn to be part of a team, win and lose, and manage their time — all skills necessary for a young woman to achieve her potential development.

At the monthly Inner Circle breakfasts, a promotional event for supporters, my efforts on behalf of student athletes are richly rewarded when an alumna of the program recounts how sport has been the defining element of her success. With each talk, I inwardly rejoice that I have the worldly goods to satisfy my innate sense of justice, which drives me to fund women's quest for equal opportunity.

What have I learned from writing my story? To bring about change within the social, political, educational, religious, and economic spheres of society has taken a longer time and a greater effort on the part of women than we initially thought. Originally, we looked forward to a progression of successful changes that would lead to our ultimate goal of equality. In actuality, we have taken two steps forward and one step back.

We know, however, that it is impossible to change a social culture without leaders, followers, and a political and social strategy — and that you need financial resources to reach your goal. Women have made progress in achieving equity through the passage of laws, which are often introduced by women legislators. To get the laws passed, there must be a critical mass of women to vote for women politicians who support their goals, and women candidates must have the money to win elections. The task of making sure those laws are implemented has been taken on by courageous women who went into court to challenge the lack of their enforcement.

As women have entered the workforce, the number of volunteers has decreased. The singleness of purpose, such as when women worked for the ERA, that I found so exhilarating as a volunteer has vanished. Women's opportunities have multiplied in many areas of society and that is a sign of success; nevertheless, I miss the original verve that was so characteristic of the early movement.

Whereas the number of women participating in the secular world has increased, within the world of the Roman Catholic Church the traditional role of women as subservient to the power of the clergy continues unabated. The power in the church lies within the ordained ministry. Women religious and laywomen are in administrative positions, but none are ordained.

The women's movement, to continue its advancement, requires an ever-increasing number of women who have the education and skills to compete in every facet of our community. There is no better way to learn to compete, function within a team, and build self-esteem than through athletics. Men start this development early on, through Little League and other sport teams. Women must continue to join the men as volunteers and foster sports for both girls and boys in playground programs. At last, the media are recognizing that women are in sports, giving us more coverage on the sports page. The Final Four women's basketball games are sellouts and television covers all four games. Women athletes are joining the male ranks as they are paid to endorse products from well-known manufacturers.

We have broken down barriers and shattered traditions. My husband has become an excellent dishwasher, supermarket shopper, and cook of a simple meal — all done with a sense of humor. My sons do the laundry. My granddaughters have been active in sports. Allison Ridder played ice hockey on the Colgate University team and was one of the five women plaintiffs in the case that elevated women's ice hockey from club status to a varsity sport. Kate Crampton played basketball at her high school. Every female, as well as male, spouse in the family works.

What excites me is how women have dared to change the customs that have governed their lives. With the barriers down, women have seized the opportunities to redefine their lives, but not without the realization that these new existences still bear the responsibilities of being a wife and mother. We adjust, improvise, and are requited for our actions.

What are the rewards we have received as a result of taking the bull by the horns? We have been part of a great movement in history, an important social revolution of the twentieth century. We have lobbied Congress and the state legislature on behalf of the women's agenda; worked for women candidates to be elected to office; run for party endorsement; and been appointed to various boards and commissions. And we have seen how women now have a greater understanding of the power of money as more and more funds are raised for women's causes.

Because I have free time and money, I have more of a responsibility to use my talents and resources to further the cause of equality for women. It always amazes me that men of means, without being criticized for it, support political candidates who protect their interests, give to causes indicative of their ambitions, and build networks that enhance their economic status. It comes naturally to these men to perform in this manner. But many women still appear fearful about giving to women's causes. I long for the day when we women not only give willingly but have numerous solicitors for our endeavors.

Sometimes I see the glass half empty, sometimes half filled. But I have to temper my pride in our progress with the realization that there is still a long way to go. For when all is said and done, the cliché "Rome wasn't built in a day" is as applicable to social change as it is to urban construction. I will continue to add building blocks to the ultimate tower of equality with the joy and passion Willa Cather so aptly describes in *My Ántonia:* "That is happiness; to be dissolved into something complete and great."

≈

Acknowledgments

I am most grateful to the many people who have responded graciously to my requests for information about organizations, people, and legislation. In particular, I want to thank my partner, Gladys Brooks, Marilyn Bryant, Walter Klaus, Elizabeth Lampland, Mary Jo Richardson, Barbara Stuhler, Sue Sattel, Gerald Stelzel, and Chris Voelz.

The Urban League, Breck School, the Minnesota Women's Political Caucus, and Senator Dave Durenberger's office permitted me to do research in their files, and to these organizations I extend my gratitude. The city of Mendota Heights, the Metropolitan Council, and the Minnesota Historical Society uncovered information, and the St. Paul Public Library reference librarians never failed to come up with a spelling, fact, or date.

I am indebted to Diedre Pope, Dorothy Rader, and George Ann Biros, who assisted along the way. To Mary Byers, who meticulously edited the manuscript, and Ann Regan, managing editor at the Minnesota Historical Society Press, who oversaw the endless details that go into publishing a book, I give my heartfelt thanks.

Jean Brookins, retired assistant director of the Historical Society for Publications and Research, *believed* that I could write this autobiography. Without her enthusiastic support, I would have foundered along the way. She patiently taught me to write, and in doing so opened a new venture that has given me great satisfaction. I cannot thank her enough.

Finally, to my husband and children, you were always there with encouragement when I suffered my emotional ups and downs as I reworked the manuscript yet another time.

Printed in the USA
CPSIA information can be obtained
at www.ICGtesting.com
JSHW082202140824
68134JS00014B/375